BRITAIN'S TRADITIONAL TRAMWAYS

BRITAIN'S TRADITIONAL TRAMWAYS

David Gladwin

BREWIN BOOKS

Published by Brewin Books Ltd
Studley, Warwickshire B80 7LG
in 2004

www.brewinbooks.com

ISBN 1 85858 250 4

British Library Cataloguing in Publication Data
A Catalogue record for this book is available from the British Library.

Typeset in Garamond
Printed in Great Britain by
Alden Press Limited

CONTENTS

ACKNOWLEDGEMENTS

All illustrations are individually acknowledged where I am aware of, or have been able to trace, the photographer. Inevitably in 50 years of collecting photographs many have been 'swops' or presents and no copyright problems arose; if any have not been acknowledged correctly my apologies. Upon notice this will be corrected in future editions.

Among those who delved into their collections for me I must specifically mention: Eric Birch, Alan Brotchie, J. Copland, Alan B. Cross, Peter Davey, John C. Gillham, Daniel Hill, H.E. Jordan, R.W. Kidner, J.S. King, John H. Meredith, A.D. Packer, Jeff Tustin, Ian Yearsley.

To these and many other colleagues and friends I offer my thanks for assistance and information willingly given.

When Alfred Baker, the General Manager of Birmingham Corporation Tramways needed new cars to expand the service in 1905 he chose for his first 50, United Electric Car Co.Ltd. bodies with Dick Kerr motors and controllers. Originally open topped they were covered between 1911 and 1925, but 32 retained her open driver's position until the end in 1933. Strangely two cars of this class were hit and badly damaged by a tornado in June 1931. Car 262, a 1907 variant was vestibuled and thus fitted survived on the Lodge Road group of services until they closed in 1947, being scrapped that year.

THE TRADITIONAL TRAM

To define a 'traditional' British tram is difficult and the next few pages show just how varied they were.

Is it the bustle of Glasgow, Renfield Street, during the last days of this system? Here the driver of car 1319, a Cunarder, built as late as 1950, en route to his depot (Newlands) waits patiently in the normal Saturday queue. Coming towards us is a much older 'Standard' - in the 1950s city road conditions the speed differential between old and new cars mattered little, although the relatively slow acceleration of an 1898 'Standard' could be an embarrassment.

Sheffield Corporation differed from some operators in that they had early 'blocks' of trams supplied in batches from different builders. Within the fleet numbers in the SE class delivered 1899 to 1904 (172 vehicles in all) there were examples of four outside builders plus those produced in the Tramways' workshops. This is one of the 1902 deliveries from the local firm of Cravens. Note both the cramped space for the motorman, the relatively flimsy fenders, and the curious plough lifeguard. Fitted with a top cover and (later) a driver's vestibule this car soldiered on until 1926.

One of three traditional tramcars delivered to Exeter Corporation Tramways (as their nos. 28-30) by the Brush Electrical Engineering Company during 1925, this classic tram seated 54, had 2 x 40 hp motors and rode on a Brush built, but Brill designed, 21E truck. After closure of Exeter's tramways on 19 August 1931, these cars (and others) were sold to Plymouth Corporation giving a further 12 or so years service. Originally light green and cream they became a very dignified maroon and ivory. Photographed in September 1925 on the Brush works' traverser at Loughborough.

Wolverhampton Corporation Tramways electrified their lines on the Lorain surface contact system; probably the most successful of all these types. It survived until 1921 when the overhead wires came into use but the last tram ran on shed 30 November 1928. This marvellously imposing car came from Brush in 1922 and although the olive green and gamboge livery was smart, film of the period did not like the colours!

TRAMS WITH FOUR LEGS

Although in terms of mileage horse trams were successful, nonetheless this success was only achieved with a degree of cruelty that would not be acceptable today.The sheer cost of operating horse trams involving as it did animal replacement after 4-7 years plus feed, hostlers, and stables, let alone trackwork ensured that fares could only be afforded by the lower middle classes. Working people just did not have the money and were, anyway, accustomed to walking prodigious journeys.The upper middle class - even shopkeepers, bank managers and the like - aspired to having a trap of their own either, rarely, owned outright or leased from and horsed by firms like Thomas Tilling or the Manchester Carriage Company. Like horse-buses the horse tram was just too small to be truly viable, except in certain circumstances, for example the Douglas cars. And, by the late 1870s they had reached the limit of their physical evolution.

The rural peace of the Folkestone, Hythe & Sandgate tramway, built between 1891 and 1892 is perhaps how we like to think of horse tramways. They never reached Folkestone but in 1893, the South Eastern Railway which was already a part owner absorbed the company running it until 1914 and again from 1919-21, when the line closed.An interesting sidelight on operating difficulties was the provision of a water tank on each of the five cars to lubricate the wheels on tight turns.

The single deck, usually one-man-operated car, was known in London as 'The Penny Bumper' as the fare was normally paid in 1d (0.4p) stages of, perhaps, a half or one mile. Car No.11 seems to be on an Aldgate service and the photograph is also of interest for the street furniture (lights, gents toilets, bollards) the other vehicles including a horse bus and the people: is the one on the left a child looking for someone's dropped penny? People seem to casually stand in the road. In Croydon where one is exhorted to dine at Neville's, High Street, South Norwood, "for a Good and cheap dinner" the interest lies at least partly in the trackwork, and especially the passing loop.

By contrast this page shows cars from the Douglas, Isle of Man, Corporation fleet, which happily still provides a horse drawn tram service in Douglas; although like many such innocent activities it is always under threat whether from "cars are best" drivers wanting all the space on the road or the 'Save-the-horse' souls. In numerical order: 42 was built by Milnes-Voss as a 32 seater in 1905; 44 came from the United Car in 1907 as a so-called 'bulkhead' car seating 40, although it was used as the Royal tram; 46 was ordered from Milnes-Voss as another bulkhead car a year later, the running boards for fare collection are apparent, in 1987 this tram was on loan to the Parks Department and used as a children's theatre.

As a final look at the horse tram scene we can revert again to the cityscapes. Perhaps the most noticeable impression is how well maintained the cars look, many used improbable colours like white, cream or sunshine yellow. But we should never forget that in these conditions if the horses lived (and many literally fell or suffered 'burst heart') they could only work between 4 and 7 years.

▲ Croydon. Note the horses are steering the tram through the rail junction.

◄ Market Street, Manchester.

▼ Exeter. Unusually, the crew are both uniformed.

▲ Liverpool. Sunshades, not umbrellas.

▲ Gravesend, Kent. Was this the first day or the last?

▲ London E4. The destination boards suggest Tooting and Waterloo Station as the terminal points. Salmon and Gluckstein were, in many ways, the forerunners of today's Tescos and Sainsburys.

▲ This was the uniform of a horse tram driver around 1890. Contrast with later electrics - but at least you were not staring at a horses -er - tail all day!

PRECURSORS

Although experiments with electrically propelled tramcars were being carried out as early as 1879, nonetheless it was not until the turn of the century that growth mushroomed. In the meantime methods other than horses were tried for tramcar propulsion.

CABLE

This cable car, which connected with horse trams to give a through service, is seen in 1899. The basic principle is that a number of endless multi-stranded steel cables, supported and guided by pulley-wheels ran at depth of between eight or nine inches in specially designed iron conduits or tubes placed centrally between the running rails. These cables were ingeniously operated by a huge 11 ft (3.35m diameter) steam-driven winch, giving a running speed of between 8 and 12 miles (13-19 km) per hour. The skill of the 'gripman' showed in his ability to not only engage and disengage his grip at passengers' requests, but to change from one cable to another. For the first London service, Telford Avenue, Streatham, to Water Lane, an endless cable 30,000 ft long (9144m) and 3 5/8" (92 mm) in circumference was required for the 2¾ miles (4.4 km) of trackwork.

The extension from Water Lane to Kennington required a 5½ mile long (8.85 km) cable which was dragged through the streets by traction engines. Operations began on 7 December 1892 although on 13 December a cable problem caused a 24-hour haitus! The line was later taken through to the Tate Library, Streatham - then a village just over 6 miles away.

In 1899 - hence the newly painted car - the London County Council took over trams in their area. The service finished 5 April 1904, pending electrification.

ALSO RANS

These two pages include a selection drawn from the multitude of unusual cars and methods of propulsion that have been operated from time to time. They are all shown in date order.

◂ No.6 of a fleet of 20 seat cars which ran for a short while from Gravesend to Northfleet in 1889. Bodies and trucks were supplied by the Falcon Car & Engineering Co.Ltd with Ewell Parker motors. Power was by the Series Electrical Traction System which promised economy, but 1889 was too early.

▴ Blackpool tried a very ingenious conduit system long before overhead electric trams had really got under way. This photograph is dated 17 December 1891, although the 1¾ miles long tramway opened 1885. Purchased by the Blackpool Corporation in 1892, orthodox overhead wiring replaced the conduit seven years later. This is probably Milnes Car No.10, fitted with ECC motors running not in a truck but as shown in trunnions.

Below & middle, two trials, with the same objective, both photographed in June 1892. Birmingham Central Tramways had a number of problems with their steam services who attracted vehement and influential opposition. They therefore tried a number of alternatives so much so that in their later guise as a B.E.T. company, City of Birmingham Tramways Company, in 1904 a breakdown showed:

CABLE: 54 cars for 3 miles
ELECTRIC (BATTERY): 24 cars for 3.82 miles
STEAM: 89 engines plus 76 trailers for 16.06 miles
HORSE: 596 horses for 10 trams and 45 buses for 2.18 miles of tramway

Not including management there were 1,177 employees.

◂ The problems inherent in battery traction are obvious from the reaction of the fumes on the paintwork.The batteries in glass cases lived under the seats.

▸ The Julien was a more attractive idea except like steam tram engines a reversing "Y" was required at each terminal point for the power car and its trailer to be turned around.

◂ The Morecambe area ended up with two distinctly 'different' forms of transport - the last horse drawn cars in regular service on the mainland: these belonged to the Corporation. Four Leyland engined petrol trams were built by UEC in 1911 for a private company, entering service on the 5th of January 1912. The line closed, mainly as these cars were worn out, on 24 October 1924. [R.W. Kidner]

STEAM TRAMS

Relatively successful in a number of areas including North Birmingham, Dudley and the hilly districts of Lancashire, the saving in running costs between horse and steam was to the order of 70%, and although the prime cost of engines was higher their ability to move 66-70 seat trailers (carrying perhaps 100+ passengers) more than outweighed this in revenue terms. Surprisingly, when new one complaint was of their relative silence; but the coke fumes from the chimney were, by all accounts, pretty foul.

▲ North London Tramways Company: the only steam tram operator in London.The engine was built by Merryweather (of steam fire pump fame) for the Great Exhibition of 1885 when it received a gold medal. The service opened 1885 but 'carriage folk' had the line closed in 1891 when horses were reintroduced.

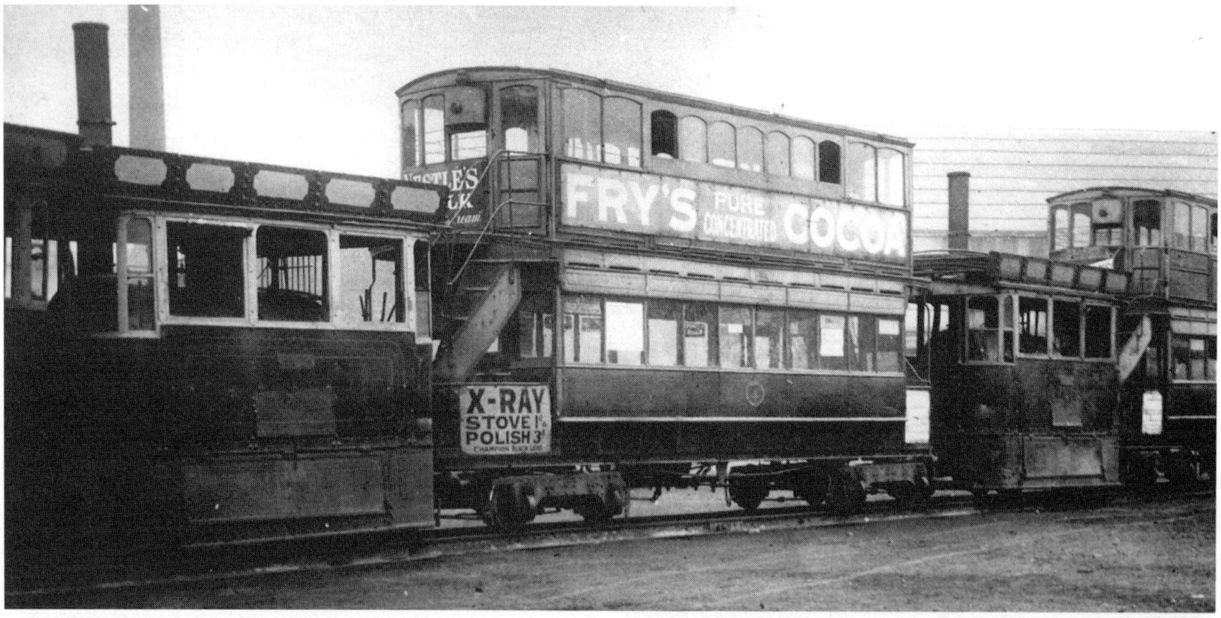

▲ Accrington Corporation Steam Tramway. Trailers were 30' long, seating as here 68-70. The missing windows upstairs were as the result of a Board of Trade directive required 'apertures' on narrow 4'0" gauge cars as they might be blown over. Engines were built by Thomas Green & Son of Leeds. Opened 1886, closed 1907.

▲ Burnley & District Tramways Company operated just over seven miles (11.26km) of trackwork from Padiham to Nelson via Burnley. Their first engines were built by Kitson of Leeds in 1881 but later more powerful machines as seen here were built by the Falcon Car & Engine Works, Loughborough (later Brush/G.E.C.) between 1883 and 1897, the line closing in 1901.The pipes on the locomotive's roof are the condensing apparatus for removing the steam normally emitted by any steam engine. Cooled, this was returned to the water tank.

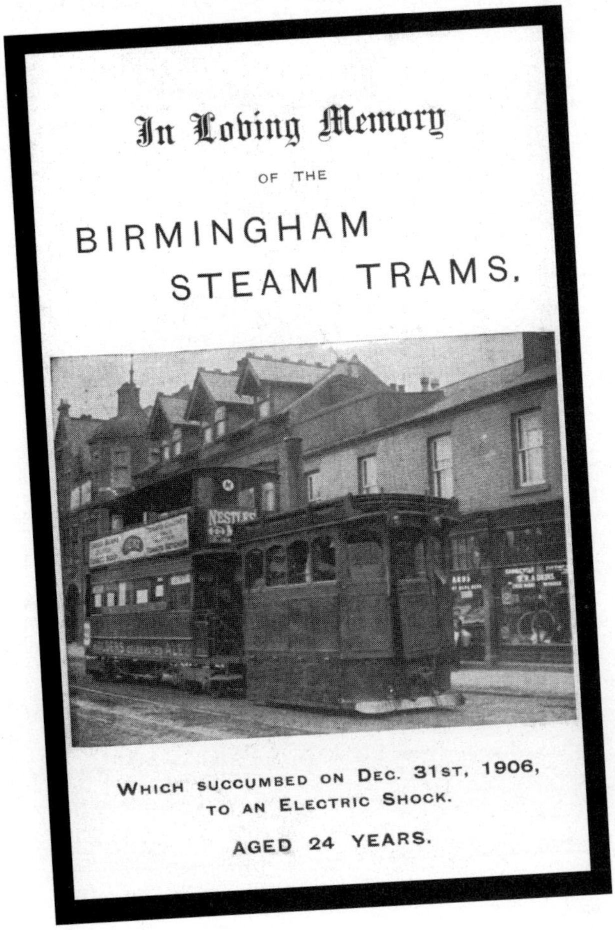

▲ Birmingham, Old Square. The postcard is dated 13 October 1920 long after the trams had gone. Was Newbury's later Lewis's?

◂ To the point!

ELECTRIC CARS - THEIR BUILDING

CONTRACTORS

A number of contractors were willing to supply complete tramway systems, although they would normally sub-contract a high percentage of the work.

As an example although Bruce Peebles were the chosen contractors for the Falkirk system and carried out the civil engineering works, having no bodybuilding facilities they only provided the motors and control gear for the tramcars.

All these concerns advertized heavily as the work was well worth undertaking.

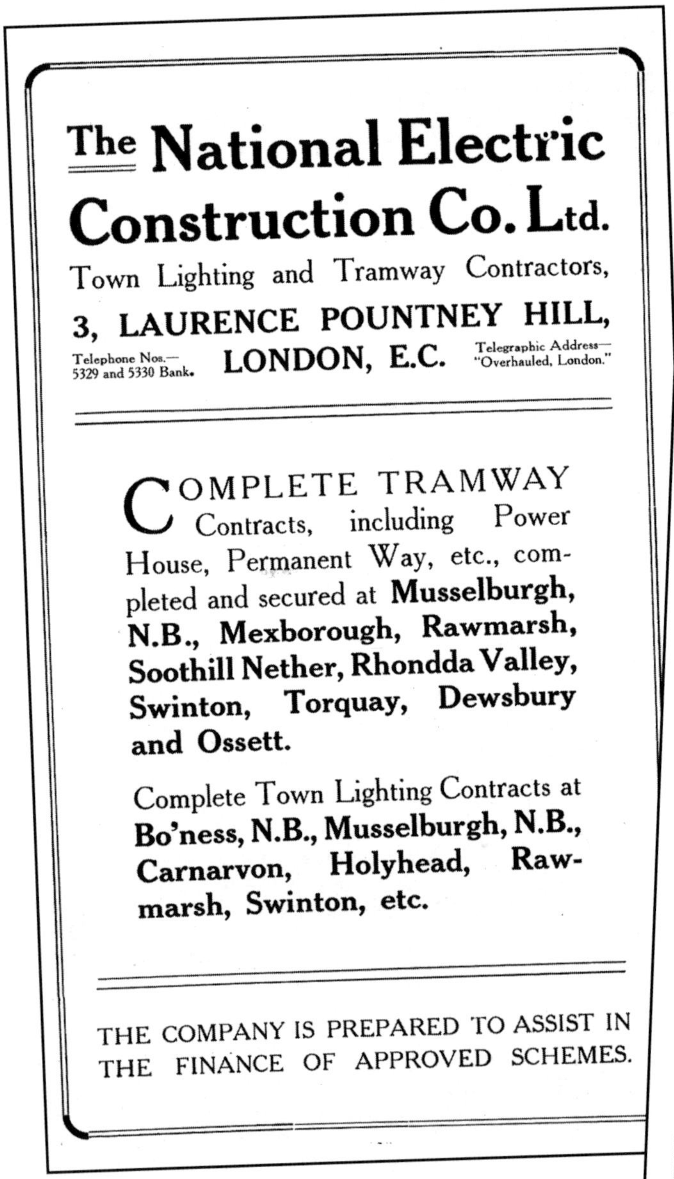

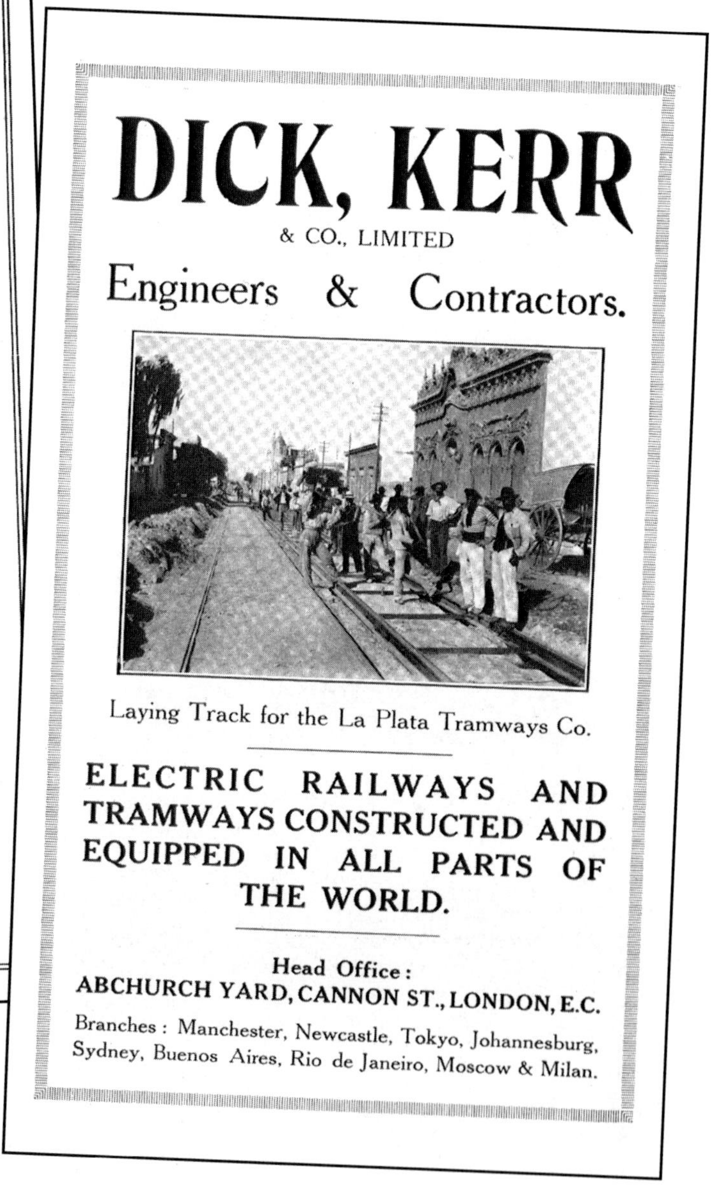

NATIONAL ELECTRIC and
DICK KERR advertisements c.1901

TRAMWAY RAIL SECTION

Obviously, this book is not intended to be a treatise on tramway engineering, but it is a salutory thought that for all of today's 'cleverness' and engineering knowledge even now not all the problems have been solved in either 'light' or 'heavy' railway applications - corrugated track still exists, railjoints still fail, and rails still 'pump' when foundations fail; failures that occur for no apparent reason. This, however, is the profile of a perfect tram rail.

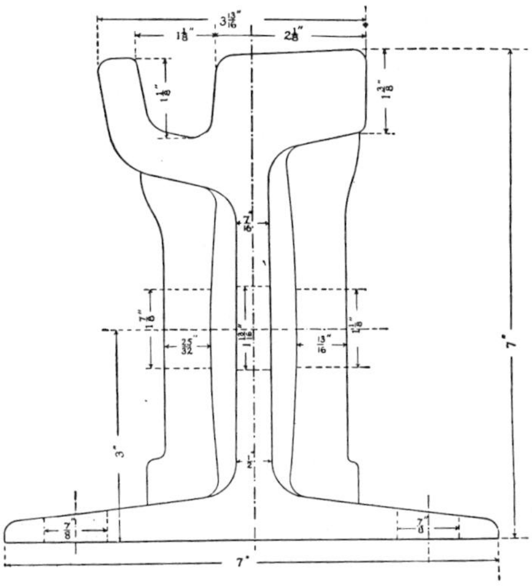

ACCRINGTON

Peel Street, September 1907, with the lines still in the process of being laid. A shelter was later erected by the lay-by, while the lines continue ahead to a junction at Abbey Street. The piles of setts on the right foretell a few weeks work for the paviors, two of whom were later to be employed full time by the Corporation. Hadfield's of Sheffield supplied the pointwork, crossings, special trackwork (as seen here) and tie bars for £5,340. At that time the manager of the system was paid £200 per annum.

Accrington trams were built to the common-to-Lancashire 4'0" gauge (1.22m) following their steam predecessors. The line to Oswaldtwistle was opened by the Mayoress on 2 August 1907, using car 4, which coincidentally is both the car to the right of the rebuilt depot in Ellison Street (seen the month previously) and that used on the first day of public services.

The 'uniform' clothing of the workmen is of note and clearly tracklaying was unfinished.

SCOTTISH INTERLUDE

For no apparent reason tram building in Scotland was unusually well recorded - particularly so when we consider the bulkiness of the photographers equipment and that a hundred years ago with the apallingly long exposure times required to expose the glass plates bright sunshine was almost essential - and not always available!

▲ Bruce Peebles were the main contractors at Falkirk, whose tramways opened 21 October 1905 with, unusually, fifteen French built trams, although as late as 1934 they were buying good second-hand cars, closure came 21 July 1936.

▲ A Balfour Beatty gang at work on the main line of Dunfermline & District's tramways. Photographed 17 September 1909 for some reason the work looks rather desultory. Opened as late as November 1909, the trams only ran until 1937.

◂ The Dundee, Broughty Ferry & District Tramway Company's main line opened in December 1905, just in time for Hogmanay. Connecting with Dundee City lines at Craigie Terrace, the service operated via Broughty Ferry to Monifieth; although a relatively poorly populated route, the Company cheerfully boasted their line was "Scotland's most beautiful tramway". This photograph shows the work in hand to strengthen and widen the bridge over the Dighty Water near Milton. The last trams ran in May 1931.

TORQUAY

1906, and the workmen take a break from laying this 3'6" (107mm) gauge tram system. In the left foreground can be seen one of the main feeder cables where obviously the concrete has been broken out to identify a fault. The bricks cover the yet to be energised studs used in the Dolter system, whereby magnets formed a circuit which then lifted the live studs into contact with a skate underslung from the truck frame. Theoretically the skate or collector shoe was always above two or more studs giving a continuous flow of power. On another similar system movement at night was described as "travelling over sheets of fire", with static and the smell of ozone two of the by-products. A more orthodox overhead system was installed in 1911.

CROSSINGS

Any railed system will, inevitably, require one or more junctions or crossings en route; even the simplest line needs to have passing loops (much as a narrow lane will have pass- bys) but clearly in a city or town these arrangements can be complex.

◂ In this photograph of a Birmingham junction we are standing on Lozells Road, Birchfield Road to our left, High Street off in the top right, Witton Road top left and Victoria Road straight ahead. Now, of course, Birchfield Road/High Street is the A34 passing under a massive roundabout feeding Lozells, Witton and Victoria roads.

▴The 8½ route miles (13.6 km) of York's electric tramways were built to narrow (3'6"/107 cm) gauge and opened in stages from January 1910. For the last 1½ years of its life until November 1935 the service was operated by a joint committee of the main bus operator, West Yorkshire Road Car, and the Corporation - a rare occurance. The building shambles at Bootham Bar Junction does not seem to 'go' with York's purported calm, the battles between conservationists and the corporation in the first decade of the 20th century over the tramways' routes were redolent of the road v. conservation confrontations in the 1990s.

▲ Paisley's tramways nearly became part of the B.E.T. empire but vacillation by the existing horse tram company and the council (who had the right to purchase in 1902) led to their abandoning their scheme in 1900. Eventually a private entrepreneur, W.M. Murphy, obtained as Act of Parliament to commence work. This photograph shows track-laying in progress near Paisley Cross during early 1904; the line to Glasgow was tested on 28 March that year, services commencing almost immediately.

▸ Although a worn photograph it not only shows one of the more complex tramway crossings but was posted from Newcastle-on-Tyne to Easingwold on 23 May 1906 and bears the comment: "This picture was taken before they paved the street. The trams are now running over this corner. Isn't Shields slow? The trams were talked of about 6 years ago, but we have got them at last". The South Shields system was opened 30 March 1906. The photograph was probably taken from the railway bridge and looks forward to Dean Road. Laygate is on the left, Stanhope Road curves away to the right. The length of roadway ripped up is amazing and must have caused chaos to local trade.

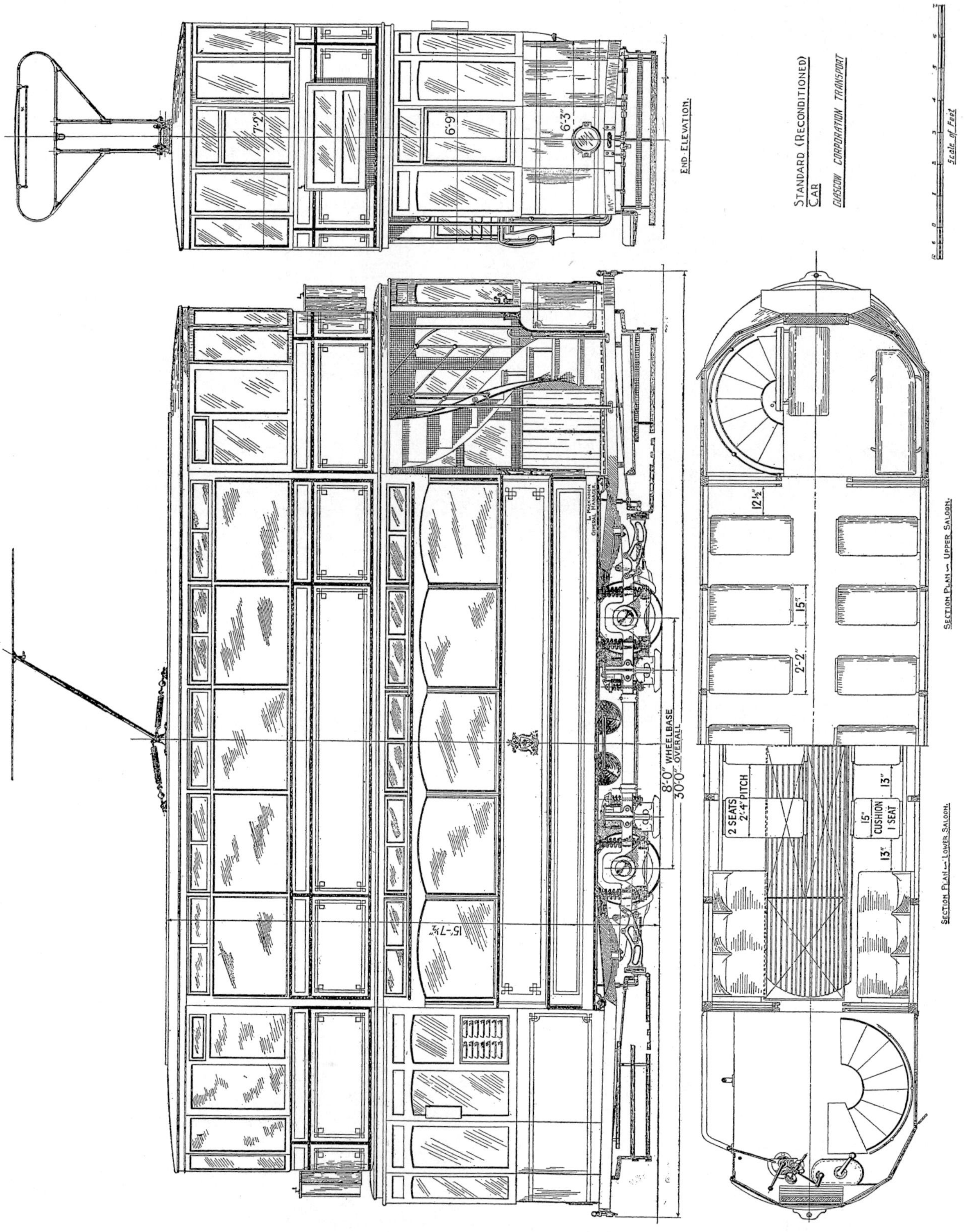

In the 1930s L. Mackinnon, the General Manager of Glasgow Corporation Transport ordered that a set of tramcar drawings be issued: years later these were still available for new motormen. This shows a Standard Car after reconditioning. Even when 'standardized', design variations still occurred, not least in the dash area. However the basic car had probably been built well before World War 1 without any vestibule or top-cover and is seen after two major rebuilds in the mid-1920s and early 1930s. After service in World War II these by now venerable cars were still to be found either plodding or gallumpting on to the end of the 1950s.

ELECTRIC LIGHT FITTINGS

No. **2051.** **18**/- each. Lamps extra.
Cast Clarus Aluminium Metal Frame, Plated Reflector, with Lamp Holder.

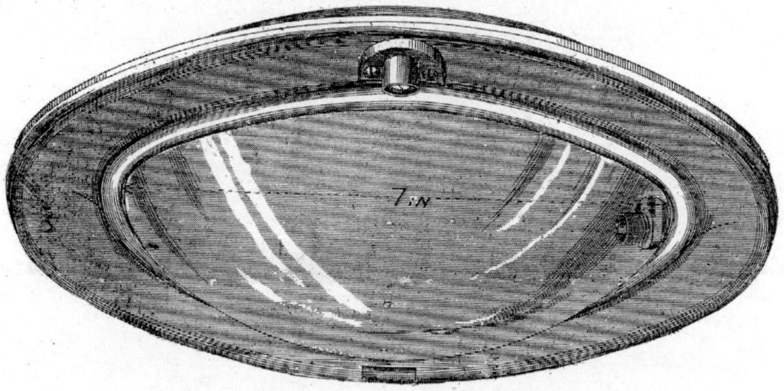

No. **2054.** **16/-** each. Lamps extra.
Cast Clarus Aluminium Metal, Porcelain Enamelled Reflector, with Lamp Holder.

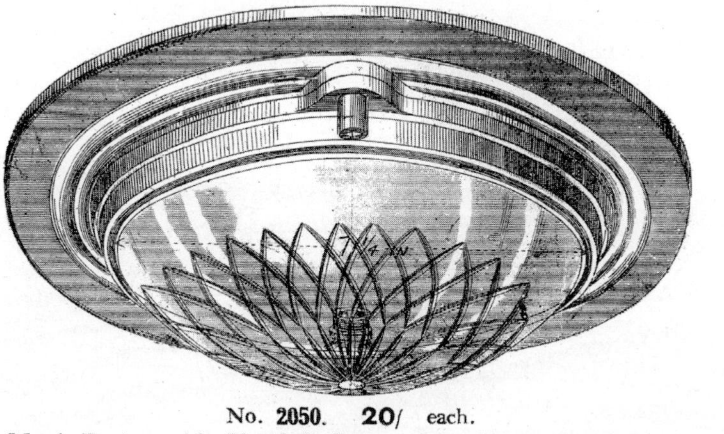

No. **2050.** **20/** each.
Cast Clarus Metal Frame, with Plated Reflector, Spun Pattress, and Lamp Holder.

Manufactured by GABRIEL & CO., BIRMINGHAM.

One of the many Birmingham companies to make a speciality of the smaller tram components, Gabriel and company had their works in A B Row; itself an oddity, with one side (A) in Aston and the other (B) in Birmingham; a few tramways had one pair of lines in one borough, the other (with different levels of rates) within next door's sphere of influence!

TRAMS ON THE MOVE

▲ These, believe it or not, are tramcars. They are being hauled by a London & North Western Railway locomotive en route to Oldham Corporation who in 1901 received delivery of twelve single deck 36 seat tramcars (11 are visible here, each 35'/107m long) from the Electric Railway & Tramway Carriage Works Ltd., at Preston, at a cost per tram, including delivery, of £950 each.

▲ Dundee Corporation Tramways opened their electrified lines on 13 July 1900 but were so successful with their first 48 trams that in 1902 these six single deck powerful bogie cars (fleet 49-54) were ordered from Hurst Nelson of Motherwell for the steeply graded line to Hilltown via Constitution and Barrack Roads. The locomotive is Caledonian Railway No. 739 complete with bearded, and proud, driver.

TRAMCARS ON SHED

Although offered in roughly completion order this collection of photographs shows Britain's traditional tramways "all shining with newth" (as a niece commented when at the East Anglian Tramways Museum, Lowestoft). But how proud the men concerned must have been after the trials and tribulations involved in building a tramway. And, too, in those days to have a husband work on a tramway or railway conveyed some prestige on his wife ...

▲ ▼ Torquay. Two faded contemporary postcards showing the new tram shed and power station being built, together with the lower deck of car 11 on its horsedrawn lurry. Sheeted over are other bodies while work continues around them. Eighteen trams were provided by Brush for the opening of the 9.24 mile (14.87 km) system on 4 April 1907.

▲ Manchester, Queens Road depot in 1904. The interest in this lies not only in the line-up of shiny almost new tramcars but also that Queens Road today houses one of the best people-friendly transport museums in the country, the Manchester Museum of Transport. Visible cars are from left to right; 250 (Brush 4 wheel 1903) 204 (Brush bogie 1903) 107 (Brush 4 wheel 1901) 141 (Brush 4 wheel 1901).

▲ Leyton Urban District Council like so many others were fiercely parochial and proud of their 'patch'. Their depot was situated in Lea Bridge Road, west of the 'Bakers Arms'; routes ran to Epping Forest ('Rising Sun'), Whipps Cross, Wanstead, and eventually Aldgate. Even after operations were taken over by the London County Council in 1921 (15 years after this photograph) 50 new trams at a cost of £145,812 were bought in 1930, although painted in LCC livery nonetheless the Leyton coat-of-arms was carried to show they were not suborned into the monolithic concern. Visible trams were supplied by Milnes, Voss with M & G radial trucks and rather enfeebled Westinghouse 200 motors.

▸ Carmuirs Depot of the Falkirk & District Traction Company photographed 21 October 1905, the day the tramway opened. Unusually the trams were built by the Compagnie Generale de Construction, St. Denis, Paris, the 4'0"/1219mm trucks, as shown, by Etablissements Arbel Forges, Douai, and the motors came from the Budapest factory of the Ganz Electric Company; although they were supplied by the contractor, Bruce Peebles & Co., Edinburgh. They survived until 1929, and the system until 1936. ▾

◂ Surprisingly gaunt two Leeds cars are seen in 1905. The general paraphernalia would give a modern safety officer a fit (but most tramway operations did and do). The scrollwork on the right hand car is typical of the period.

◂ Although the renowned Glasgow Corporation Transport works at Coplawhill from time to time suffered from the Great British Disease of industrial action, often due to causes that fifty years on seem hard to understand, nonetheless their output of new and refurbished cars was a tribute to all the men and women involved; the shame is that now we have so little to show of this once marvellous fleet that served the city so well. As this photograph is dated 1950 these three cars are probably 'Cunarders' 1348-50, destroyed in their prime 1962. Alongside (left) is a 'Coronation' and behind an early 'Standard'.

▾ Part of Weston-super-Mare's fleet is seen inside the Locking Road depot. Two types of cars are shown, the orthodox 3-bay Brush four wheelers, open topped and no protection for the motorman. In November 1912 residents sent a petition to the Board of Directors asking for glass screens to protect the men. "No", answered the Manager, "but we'll give them a set of oilskins". Two crossbench open sided cars are also visible, the nearest built 1902, the one at the rear 1927. The overhead tower lurks on the right. [The late F. White]

OPENING CEREMONIES

▲ Opening ceremonies were curiously varied. This is the car No.86 of class "A" used by the London County Council Tramways for the Royal opening of the lines to Tooting, Friday, 15 May 1903.

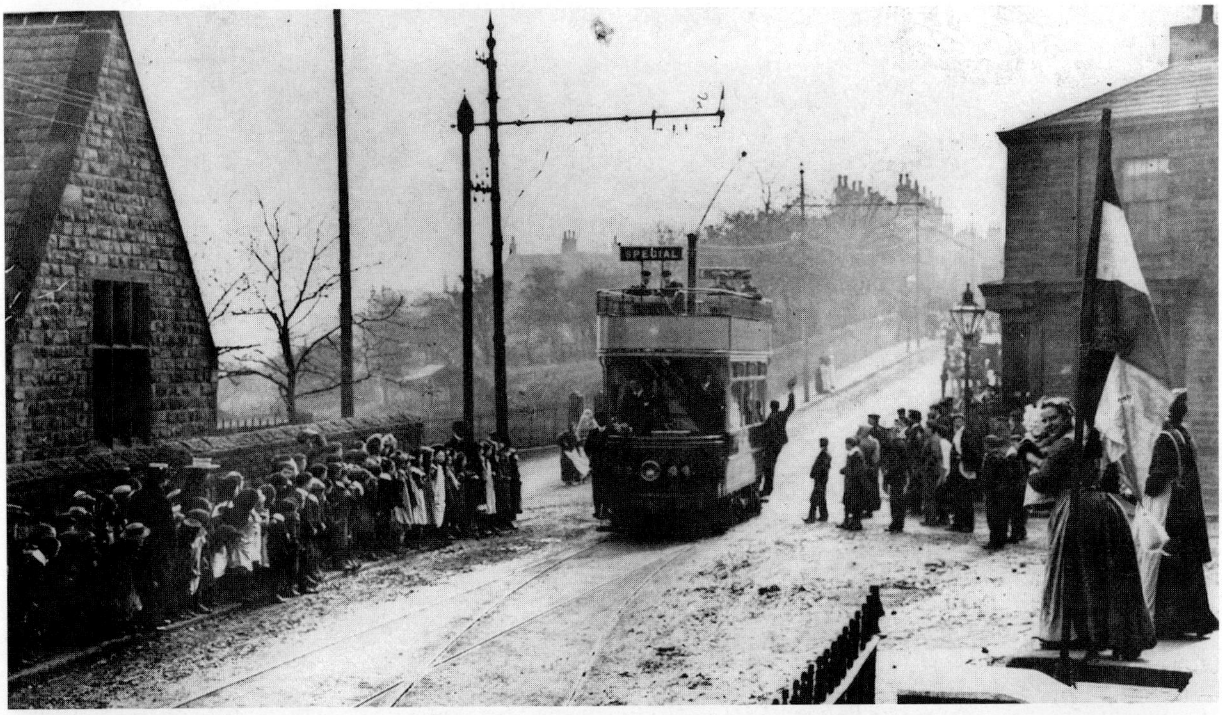

▲ By contrast when the new lines extending the Yorkshire Woollen District cars to Gomersal were opened on 2 October 1905, although the schools emptied, the car was not decorated at all. The condition of the road is typical for the period.

▲ Colchester decided to really put on a show on 28 July 1904 - pity it was a normal summer's day!

▼ The Airdrie and Coatbridge Tramways Company mustered the notables of the area on 8 February 1904, but you cannot really blame them for wearing heavy warm clothing in a Scottish February! The ladies had their time later in the day.

BIRMINGHAM INTERLUDE

Birmingham trams, until their slaughter, showed the slow and steady progression of the traditional tramcar: most notable for their colouring, blue and cream of the richest hues and incomparable maintenance. All gone of course except one lonely car encapsulated in a museum.

▲ Once a depot and later a bus garage where the Cotteridge tram 817 stands is now a block of flats. This photograph shows how gaunt these narrow gauge cars really were. 817 of the 'M & T air-brake' class had bodywork by Short Brothers (of Rochester) who were not very busy building aircraft in 1928, and the trucks and their braking systems came from Maley & Taunton. Delivered in 1929 upholstered transverse seating was provided, the cars having an overall height of 15'10½" (4.84m) while weighing 16.75 tons. Seating 60, this car was withdrawn upon closure of the Bristol Road group of services, and scrapped July 1951. [J.Tustin]

▲ Kyotts Lake was the Birmingham Corporation Tramways overhaul depot and 628 is seen bereft of its bogies in the late 1930s. Built in 1920 this car was typical of its type when delivered as part of a batch of 50, with Brush bodywork and trucks, seating 62, 28 on longitudinal benches in the lower saloon and 34 on transverse wooden seats upstairs. The length of the saloon between corner pillars was 21' (6.4m) over the fenders 33'6" (10.2m) and, being on narrow gauge rails an overall width of 6'3" (1.9m). This class of tram was gradually updated in equipment and fittings, including upholstered transverse seating giving a final capacity of 63. Although 'our' 628 was broken up in November 1950, one of the class (616) was Birmingham's official last car.

▾ Pure tradition and pure pride of ownership. The lettering on this tramcar tells the ratepayers to be aware they have the best trams in the world! A relatively low-height car, No. 163, entered service late 1906 and apart from an experimental rebuild of its failed radial truck led quite an uneventful life being updated with upholstered transverse sets and better lighting until withdrawn April 1939.

▾ The quality of this Roy Marshall photograph shows all the details of this 1923 batch of trams whose bodies were marvellously built but at a heavy loss for their manufacturer, the Midland Railway Carriage & Wagon Company, Washwood Heath, Birmingham. Powerful with 40 h.p. motors, they were fast and comfortable trams especially after seating improvements and survived until the end of Birmingham's traditional tramways. [1685 Group/Roy Marshall]

▲ 829 was one of the last (1929) cars built for BCT. Bodies by Short Brothers of Rochester and M & T air-braked bogies ensured good solid tramcars. No fancy bits, just real workmanship. Before being broken up in August 1952 all of this class averaged 710,000 miles in service.

▸ Dudley 23 October 1938, and by the sign reading "Cars load here for Oldbury, Smethwick and Birmingham", car 98 waits for departure time. The fender advertises the 'Birmingham University Hospital Carnival 1938, at the Serpentine Ground, October 28, 29, 30'. The clever dual purpose usage of the traction standard is worthy of note. Car 98 was to have been open topped but this Board of Trade rule was relaxed for most inland tramway systems. Withdrawals of this class began in May 1938, 98 following in September 1939 upon the closure of Hockley depot.

▲ Solid tradition is in car 651 built 1923, 33'6" (10.21m) long over fenders, 21' (6.4m) between the pillars of the lower deck, 6'3" (1.905m) wide, 15'6" (4.72m) high, weighing 16 tons and after "soft" cushioned seats replaced the wooden slats, 62 passengers sat in comfort. [Roy Marshall]

▲ A beautiful study of a B.C.T. car adjacent to the Railway Inn, Soho, the Lodge Road terminus, together with a suspiciously clean child (was it Sunday?), gas lamp and Bundy clock, this latter used by the driver who would insert his numbered key, press the lever (although some were automatic) which then recorded his departure time on a reel of paper. This area, which is within a few minutes walk of Winson Green prison is now almost unrecognisable although the 'Railway' was still standing, derelict and boarded up, in 1996. Car 61, as delivered, had neither top deck cover nor drivers' vestibules and was one of the first BCT cars to arrive in 1906. Seating 48, this car was supplied with a Brill 21E truck of 6' (1.83m) wheelbase. Rebuilt at various times, tops were fitted in 1911, and in 1924, 61 (as with other Lodge Road cars) received a bow collector in lieu of the usual trolley pole, the final type used by BCT (the self lubricating Rowlands skate) was supplied in 1930, this car and 15 others out of nearly 300 being retained at Rosebery Street depot until scrapped in May 1947.

▲ Two experimental cars were built for the BCT, entering service (842) in November 1929 and September 1930 (843). The last ever built for Birmingham, space precludes giving all their story but both were superb lightweights, reducing the overall weight by nearly 4½ tons. The designs might have kept the tramways open but there was no follow-up ... that was the end.

BIRMINGHAM CITY TRANSPORT

FARES

2d. Ordinary. — 1d. Children's.

Routes	Stage	BETWEEN
36 Cotteridge, 46 British Oak, 53 Dogpool	1st Stage	Navigation Street and Pebble Mill Road—Bristol Road Junction
	2nd ,,	Belgrave Road and Kitchener Road
	3rd ,,	Speedwell Road and Dogpool Lane
	4th ,,	Bristol Road—Pebble Mill Road Junction and Elm Tree Road
	5th ,,	Kitchener Road and Cotteridge Terminus
35 Selly Oak, 69 Northfield, 70 Rednal, 71 Rubery, 72 Longbridge	1st Stage	Navigation Street and Pebble Mill Road
	2nd ,,	Belgrave Road and Bournbrook Road
	3rd ,,	Speedwell Road and Chapel Lane, Selly Oak
	4th ,,	Pebble Mill Road and Weoley Park Road
	5th ,,	Bournbrook Road and Cob Lane
	6th ,,	Chapel Lane, Selly Oak, and Bell Inn, Northfield
	7th ,,	Weoley Park Road and Quarry Lane
	8th ,,	Cob Lane and Hawkesley Mill Lane
	9th ,,	Whitehill Lane and Longbridge
	10th ,,	Bell Inn, Northfield, and Lowhill Lane or Colmers Farm School, Rubery
	11th ,,	Quarry Lane and Rednal or Rubery
1 Stockland Green, 2 Erdington, 63 Tyburn Road, 78 Short Heath, 79 Pype Hayes	1st Stage	Steelhouse Lane and Aston Station
	2nd ,,	Dartmouth Street and Slade Road Junction
	3rd ,,	Aston Cross and Hunton Hill
	3rd ,,	Aston Cross and Stoneyhurst Road
	4th ,,	Aston Station and Marsh Lane
	4th ,,	Aston Station and Barnabas Road
	4th ,,	Aston Station and Bromford Lane
	5th ,,	Slade Road Junction and Station Road
	5th ,,	Slade Road Junction and Short Heath Road Terminus
	5th ,,	Slade Road Junction and Kingsbury Road—Tyburn Road Junction
	6th ,,	Hunton Hill—Gravelly Hill North Junction and Chester Road Terminus
	6th ,,	Stoneyhurst Road and Pype Hayes Terminus

3d. Ordinary. — 1½d. Children's.

Routes	Stage	Between
36 Cotteridge	1st Stage	Navigation Street and Elm Tree Road
	2nd ,,	Belgrave Road and Cotteridge Terminus
35 Selly Oak, 69 Northfield, 70 Rednal, 71 Rubery, 72 Longbridge	1st Stage	Navigation Street and Chapel Lane, Selly Oak
	2nd ,,	Belgrave Road and Cob Lane
	3rd ,,	Speedwell Road and Whitehill Lane
	4th ,,	Pebble Mill Road and Bell Inn, Northfield
	5th ,,	Bournbrook Road and Hawkesley Mill Lane
	6th ,,	Chapel Lane, Selly Oak and Longbridge
	7th ,,	Cob Lane and Rednal or Rubery
1 Stockland Green, 2 Erdington, 63 Tyburn Road, 78 Short Heath, 79 Pype Hayes	1st Stage	Steelhouse Lane and Marsh Lane
	1st ,,	Steelhouse Lane and Barnabas Road
	1st ,,	Steelhouse Lane and Bromford Lane
	2nd ,,	Dartmouth Street and Station Road
	2nd ,,	Dartmouth Street and Short Heath Road Terminus
	2nd ,,	Aston Cross and Kingsbury Road—Tyburn Road Junction
	3rd ,,	Aston Cross and Chester Road Terminus
	3rd ,,	Aston Station and Pype Hayes Terminus

4d. Ordinary. — 2d. Children's.

Routes	Stage	Between
36 Cotteridge	1st Stage	Navigation Street and Cotteridge
70 Rednal, 71 Rubery, 72 Longbridge	1st Stage	Navigation Street and Quarry Lane
	2nd ,,	Belgrave Road and Hawkesley Mill Lane
	3rd ,,	Speedwell Road and Longbridge
	4th ,,	Pebble Mill Road and Lowhill Lane or Colmers Farm School, Rubery
	5th ,,	Bournbrook Road and Rednal or Rubery
2 Erdington, 78 Short Heath, 79 Pype Hayes	1st Stage	Steelhouse Lane and Chester Road Terminus
	1st ,,	Steelhouse Lane and Short Heath Road Terminus
	1st ,,	Steelhouse Lane and Pype Hayes Terminus

5d. Ordinary. — 8d. Workmen's. — 2d. Children's.

Routes	Stage	Between
70 Rednal, 71 Rubery	1st Stage	Navigation Street and Rednal or Rubery

WORKMEN'S TICKETS

entitling the holder to make two journeys on any Tramcar during the day are issued to Passengers terminating their journey at a stage point before 9 a.m. as above, except on Sundays and on such other days as may be announced by Public Notice.

CHILDREN under FIVE years of age free, if not occupying a seat, providing that not more than one such child accompanies any passenger. Additional children irrespective of age, must be paid for. For children over FIVE years and under FOURTEEN years of age the fares are as shown above. Children over FOURTEEN and under EIGHTEEN years of age undergoing full-time education may ride at Children's Fares when on journeys between home and school or in connection with the school curriculum on presenting a Permit obtainable at the City Transport Traffic Department, Congreve Street. Hours 10-0 a.m. to 5-0 p.m., Mondays to Fridays.

All Complaints as to the Services or Servants of the Department should be addressed to

THE GENERAL MANAGER,
BIRMINGHAM CITY TRANSPORT, BIRMINGHAM.

March, 1952
TRAMS

TRAMSCAPES

To a very great degree the tramcar was a creature of urban living, with the high initial cost of trackwork, overhead wiring and the cars themselves, the only way any tramway could be made to pay was by shifting crowds around the town or city. To do this fares must be cheap, which (without subsidy) carries as a corollary a requirement for cheap electrical power and relatively low wages. In practice early years saw vast sums being drained from Corporation owned tram systems to keep rates down - even after amortizing the prime costs of the tramways returns to the council could run at 10-15% on capital expended. And if the tramway was privately (primarily B.E.T. owned) then an absolute minimum of 4% per annum was required. Less than that ... goodbye, as happened to so many tramways in the aftermath of not only the first World War, but of the General Strike. Costs rose to an unsustainable level and in very many cases not only could the infrastructure not be replaced but small, light, buses, often operated on a shoe-string by ex-servicemen could run in circles around tired and worn tramcars. But during their time trams showed people they could get out of their houses to other places and could change their jobs from the next-door mill or factory and more importantly that they could afford to do these things.

On 16 May 1950 the last Bradford Trams carried out the duties they had performed since the first steam cars in 1882. Although this is the centre of a busy industrial town there is a curious tranquillity about the scene.

▲ The changing face of a traditional tramway was never more marked than in these two photographs. The Oldham car, No.94, is standing by the Star Inn, King Street, Oldham c.1922. A very traditional tramcar 94 is only nine years old and a typical product including the truck of UEC Preston, albeit the electrical fittings are all from Siemens. The white markings on the standard indicate this is a feeder (dividing the power supply into ½ mile (800m) or less sections), the huts (two are visible) are for the use of pointsmen and inspectors as Star Inn was the hub of the system where seven sets of rails met. Gas lighting remains despite electric trams. [Oldham 94, E. Gray]

▼ The Aberdeen car, No.34, is often said to have represented the apotheosis of traditional tramcar building, but these beautiful machines had precious little chance to show their merits as delivered in 1949 they were summarily scrapped along with the tramway system in 1958. Comfortable transverse seating for 76 passengers was fitted, both of the saloons electrically heated and the fully enclosed drivers cab had, wonder of wonders, electric windscreen wipers in addition to air and hand brakes. Loudspeakers were fitted throughout the cars to enable the driver to announce the stops and, later, the doors were fitted for remote operation by him in lieu of the conductor. Current collection was by way of Fischer bow, not unlike modern railway technology. The workman behind is using a hose attached to a street (fire) hydrant to flush out the points mechanism, as even on 12 May 1956 when this photo was taken road detritus could make operation difficult. [Aberdeen car 34, M.A. Arnold]

▲ A trio of Londoners. 259 is standing underneath the ornamental bracketry of a long arm standard at North Woolwich Ferry terminus. The trackwork complexity is daunting for any engineer. 259 was built for West Ham Corporation by Brush in 1905 and broken up in 1937.

▲ 85 is an ex East Ham Corporation car (55) built by Brush to be in all main aspects identical to LCC standard E/1 trams, even having LCC class 4 bogies. This car remained in service until the last full day of London's trams, Saturday 5 July 1952, when route 72 Woolwich to Savoy Street, Strand, was converted to bus operation "to rejuvenate travel in London". Photographed near Shooters Hill Road, 28 June 1952. [R.W. Kidner]

► The embankment can rarely have looked finer than on this summer day. 169 ex Leyton Council was constructed by English Electric on EMB maximum traction trucks as an LCC E/3 class clone with more than adequate power for the 70 minute run via Westminster, Camberwell Green, New Cross, Lewisham and Woolwich Common to Beresford Square. R.W. Kidner describes earlier days, "Track condition on the LCC system was good, though one seldom had the chance to evaluate it at speed. almost the only place was the 1 mile and a quarter of reserved track on the Victoria Embankment. In the morning rush-hour of 1927 a driver seeing clear rail ahead would put on full power, being followed by other cars as fast as they were able. Often these mad rushes would be headed by one of the through-running Croydon Council cars, built by Hurst Nelson in 1926 especially for this service, and powered by two 65 hp motors. If one of the few remaining C class four-wheelers tried to keep up it soon developed a painful fore-and-aft rock. Occasionally this would cause the gate of the body-catcher to strike the ground, releasing the scoop, which would skitter along the track until the driver had pulled himself together enough to raise it".

CURRENT COLLECTION TECHNIQUES

▲ Bound for Renfrew Ferry, Glasgow, 'Standard' 543, built in August 1901, was finally scrapped in 1953, not however before this car was updated to provide a good, workmanlike, tram. In many ways this scene typifies the glory of the British traditional tram. Current collection by bow collector.

▼ Sunderland No.31 was one of eight cars bought from Huddersfield. A mere 7 years old, in tram terms they were barely run in and fitted with a pantograph by Sunderland provided a truly magnificently comfortable ride alongside the seafront, as here at Seaburn with the lights compensating for high winds and rough(ish) seas in September 1953. 31 will leave Seaburn behind her on the Circle route (actually more of a tadpole) via Bridge St., Vine Place and Hylton Road. [J. Copland]

▲ Even if we discount the electrical and physical advantages of pantograph and bow current collectors this illustration shows exactly why in today's fast moving traffic the trolley pole is no longer a viable proposition unless the cars run solely into termini which are separated from other road users. Even where museum operation is concerned absent minded visitors bounce off the conductor/guard usually as he or she bounces the trolleywheel off the overhead wire. It never was much shakes as a desirable job in mid winter with the rain dribbling down ones neck and if (as many did) the conductor wore spectacles, at night time that wire was often invisible! The open topped car is from the London United Tramways fleet. Delivered 1901, these rather under powered cars were particularly noted for their very safe 'broken' staircases which incorporated a landing.

▼ The London Transport cars are seen in 1951 running on the conduit system with their trolley poles lowered. The details of both car roofs are reasonably clear; the 'Feltham' nearest to the photographer has wooden walkways each side of the poles due to the camber of the car's roof; the fixed ventilators make it relatively cluttered, although the 'plank' under the pole is of simple construction compared with that of the E1. Route 16 (the Feltham) was a circular trip Purley-Croydon-Embankment-Purley lasting 73 minutes with a car every 3 minutes while the E.1 on route 40 took 76 minutes from Abbey Wood via Plumstead to Savoy Street, Strand.
[J.C. Gillham]

A DEGREE OF MODERNIZATION

▲ The existence of the 5.38 mile (8.66 m) long Swansea and Mumbles Railway could be traced back to 1804, with the first passenger car running as early as 1807. In 1877, as the Oystermouth Railway, it became a real mix'n'match with both horse and steam hauled trains and trams running together. The line reached its final length in 1898, but the lease eventually passed to the South Wales Transport Company in 1927 who, after electrification, reopened the service in 1929 with 13 magnificent 106-seater cars, built by Brush. Each had 2 x 60 h.p. motors with provision for multiple unit control and in peak hours two could be coupled together requiring only one driver. Through air brakes (not finally standardized on British Rail until the 1980s) gave excellent stopping ability and as pantographs were fitted no pole reversal was required at the termini. The line closed in 1960 and the cars were scrapped.

▼ A London Transport 'Feltham' bears down on the photographer in London Road, Norbury, 13 August 1949, as the track repair gang carry out some patching work. The handcart contains tools (picks, shovels and crowbars) together with 'bitza', the solid tyred trailer by the lorry is the tar boiler and the one man working is using a punner to consolidate the surface. The tree on the extreme left still has its wartime whitewash ring designed to increase its visibility during the blackout. [John H. Meredith]

▲ When these cars arrived in Blackpool they were a source of wonder to many visitors accustomed to elderly, open balcony, draughty, and sometimes rattly trams in their own area. Amazing to think 70 years on Blackpool still (2004) has a few of this class in daily service.

▼ The first Birmingham experimental car, 842, is seen at Cotteridge, the terminus of the 36 route in 1939. Built as a super-lightweight car by Short Bros. of Rochester this all metal tram consisted of aluminium alloys for the framing, roof, and upper saloon floor plus aluminium sheeting for the panels. The underframe and the dash panels however, were in steel. Seating 63 this narrow (3'6") gauge car measuring 33'6" x 6'3" overall with a height of 15'6" entered service from Cotteridge Depot in November 1929!

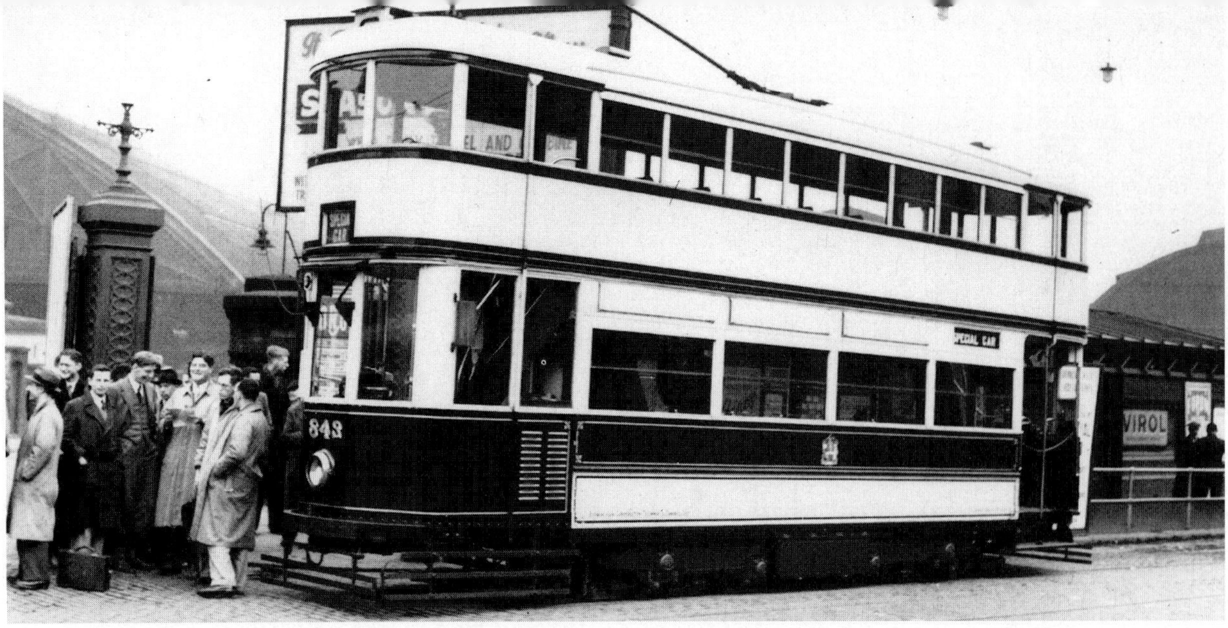

▲ In the early postwar days visiting tram systems and lines in peril of closure became an almost commonplace occupation of many young(ish) men, who like me could not understand why tramcars were doomed; other than appreciating the necessity to line the pockets of greedy men, most of us still fail to appreciate the reasoning of the City 'Fathers', of Birmingham, Sheffield, Glasgow, Sunderland and other cities. The saddest part of photographs like this one of 843 is that most of these men (and a few women) have gone off to the great tram-shed in the sky - and those remaining are getting a bit antique! [The Omnibus Society]

▼ Although Glasgow had an enormous fleet of elderly 'Standards' they also tried to find a way forward with cars built using modern techniques and modern equipment. In No.1005, seen here in monochrome, but in reality painted in three shades of blue (Prussian, Sky and Wedgwood), they tried a "thru-flow" car using, as shown, one entrance for boarding and a separate exit. Incredibly, given postwar conditions this innovative tramcar (the nearest ever attained to European-style working) was completed by 1 September 1947 - and regard how modern even today, over 50 years later, she still looks! 72 luxury seats, panoramic windows, fluorescent lighting (in the front) air operated folding doors, most of all it was single ended - just like a bus! Because it was a one-off bristling with experimental gear neither the Glasgow public or the maintenance staff really took to 1005 and in due course this lovely car was converted to a double ended hybrid, surviving thus until 1962.

▼ This magnificent photograph dated 22 November 1933 once hung on an officer's wall in Edge Lane Works, Liverpool, and depicts a type of tram long gone and which will never be duplicated. At its simplest it is a "1933 EMB bogie car built at Edge Lane to the City Electrical Engineers Instructions", but surely it is a thing of beauty: beauty allied to function. 772 was one of a batch (770-781) to first carry the striking green livery introduced in her build year and were the original 'Green Goddesses' named after the film staring George Arliss which as then popular. The bogies were the first EMB heavyweights derived from those used by LCC tramways. Alas, 772, was to be the first of her class to be scrapped on 23 September 1943 after irrepairable damage following a bombing raid in 1940.

TRACK WORKS

▲ Manchester Corporation Tramways renewal gangs at work. To the right is Portland Street, lines to St. Peters Square, and Oxford Road provide the 'main line'. Tools are primitive and one of the most tedious jobs was cleaning and fettling the thousands of granite setts recovered for further use. Manchester used to be murky from industry, now, alas, it is vehicle fumes that sully the atmosphere.

▸ Farnworth Urban District Council Tramways. An amazing complex of rails, all supplied as a kit of parts. Curiously for a UDC Farnworth, population 26,000, a suburb of Bolton, decided to erect their own generating station and lay the trackwork within the UDC boundaries. Worsley Road is ahead, Buckley Lane right, Long Causeway left and the photographer is standing near the depot above Albert Road. By 1901 the Farnworth tramways carried one-and-a-half million passengers over their roughly 5 miles (8 KM) of route network, using 13 cars.

MANCUNIAN DAYS

▸ I have deliberately made this the first photograph. It is dated 17 February 1905 and shows Manchester Corporation Tramways Parcels Van No.1. I chose it simply because I admire the crew and their stance. Would anyone be proud (or willing) to take on a job like this in the 21st century?

▾ A wonderful mélange of traffic in Manchester as car 366 on the Edge Lane-Piccadilly route passes along in 1912. 366 was built as a 4-wheel open top car by G.F. Milnes in 1902 and subsequently updated.

Although Manchester never really modernized its fleet nonetheless it did not seem possible the city could become tramless.

▲ 1901 and boskage at the opening.

◂ ▾ 1911 and all the people of an Edwardian City.

▲ 1931. In the third pane of glass can be read as in a mirror "All inward cars stop here".

▼ 1949. They did, finally. [Ian Yearsley]

BRISTOLIAN WAYS

Except for incidental details (slight changes in livery, plainer lettering and fleet numbers etc.) the photograph of car 223 might as well have been taken in 1938 as 1908. The story of Bristol's trams really goes back to the Acts of Parliament authorizing electrification of the horse tram system. The first electric cars ran on 14 October 1895 when would-be tramway managers came from all over the world to see an advanced line in use but when in 1915 Bristol Corporation could have exercised their right to take over the 31 route miles (50 km) the exigencies of war prevented this and the company, Bristol Tramways & Carriage Co.Ltd., perforce developed their bus operations as they knew that every seven years (1922, 1929, etc.) their tramway would be worth little more than scrap. The cars were however kept in immaculate condition and were sold in 1937 to the Corporation who intended to close the lines within two years, although due to the advent of (another) war and fuel rationing this did not finally happen until 11 April 1942.

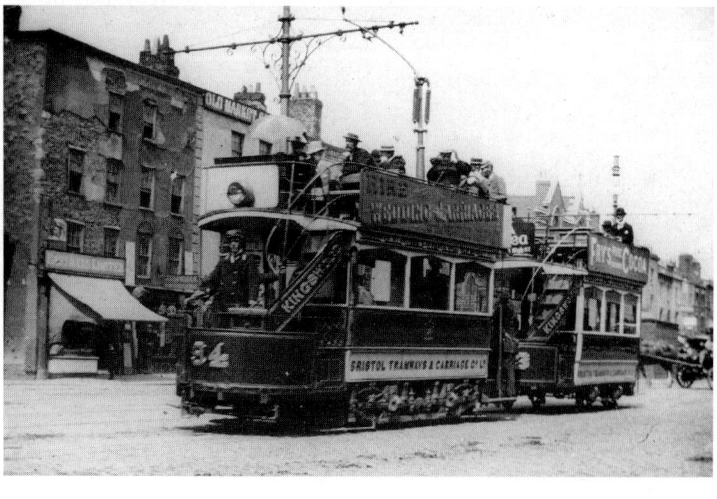

▲ ▶ Car 223 was 'home built' in 1901 on a rather rare McGuire 'Columbian' truck, while 94 (Milnes 1895, Peckham cantilever) is seen in Old Market Street towing a matching ex-horse tram, some of which remained in use until 1904, despite the delays this activity caused, the two 20 h.p motors being rather 'tishy' for the work, although 8 m.p.h. (12.87 kph) was regarded as fast in 1896, the date of the photograph.

▲ Scrolls and poles caught the eye of this photographer - the rest of the scene is, like the pole, just history. Card dated 15 September 1904.

▼ Exigencies of wartime. Rather a severe uniform but skirts have been shortened to a more practical length by 1917. Horsfield depot. [M.J. Tozer Collection]

TRAMARAMA

Many years ago another writer coined the word 'Tramarama' to describe the vision of tramcars doing what they did. These are my offerings:

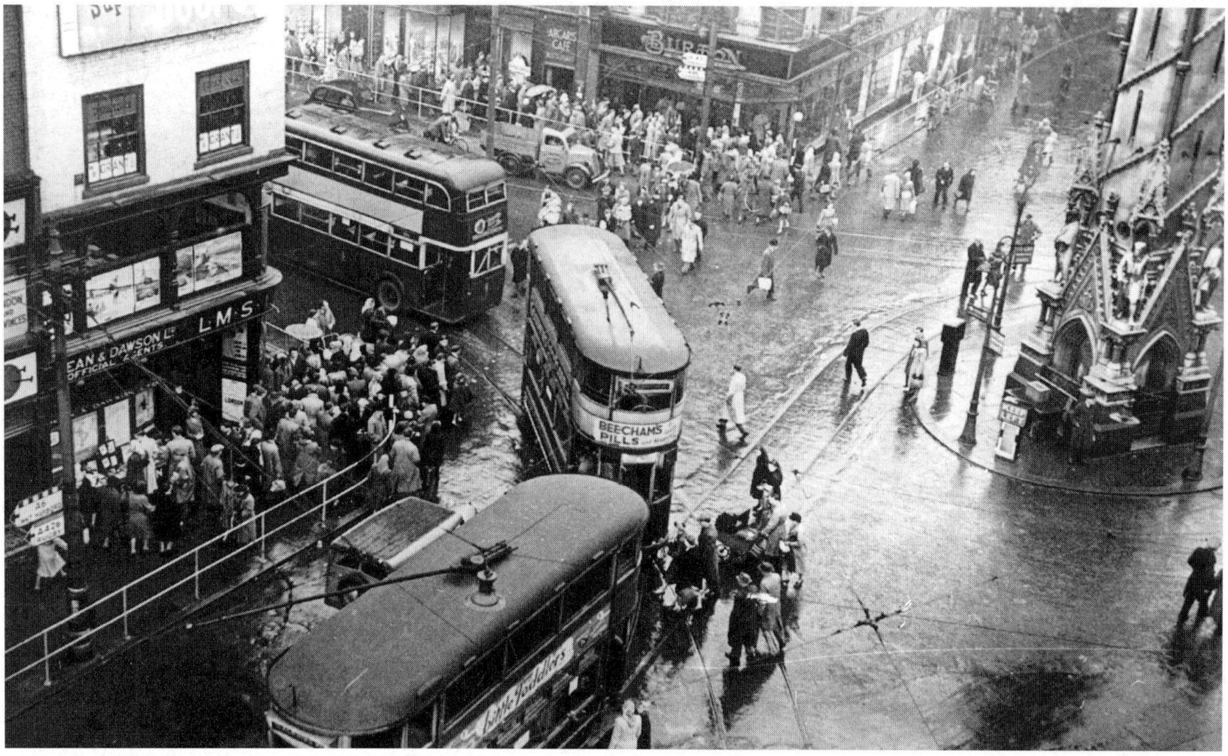

▲ Clock Tower, Leicester. Yes, it always rained!

▼ Rhondda car at the Miners' Institute.

▲ En route to Kelvingrove, tram 905 suits the buildings of Glasgow perfectly.

▸ Colchester. Stands the Church clock at ten to three? (well almost ...) And is there still honey for tea?

▼ Halifax. But at least the driver's position is vestibuled. No heaters of course! [Halifax Courier]

▲ Cockles and mussels? Perhaps not in what was (pre-refugee) genteel old Hastings.

◂ The reverse of this postcard states "Just a card as promised and I am so glad you are coming tonight ..." says it all really. 10 a.m. 28 December 1907. But this is glorious Southsea at its best.

▼ Forster Square, Bradford. Steam trams have gone and in the 1920s electric trams rule.

▲ One of my favourites simply because there is a period 'rightness' about the scene. Theatre Square, Nottingham.

▼ Worcester. The buildings in this scene were, in 2004, surprisingly unchanged.

▲ Remember Weston-super-Mare when it was a town where you went to the seaside? and "Penny Fares all the way"? And when public transport was "full and standing" with regularity?

◂ Service 42 to Alcester Lane's End. And Birmingham car 386 is passing Highgate Park, Moseley Road. Does 'the white house' still stand today?

▼ Ilford Corporation car No.10 at Ley Street, later, after being given a top cover, nicknamed 'Noah's Ark'. It was scrapped in 1920, worn out after the war.

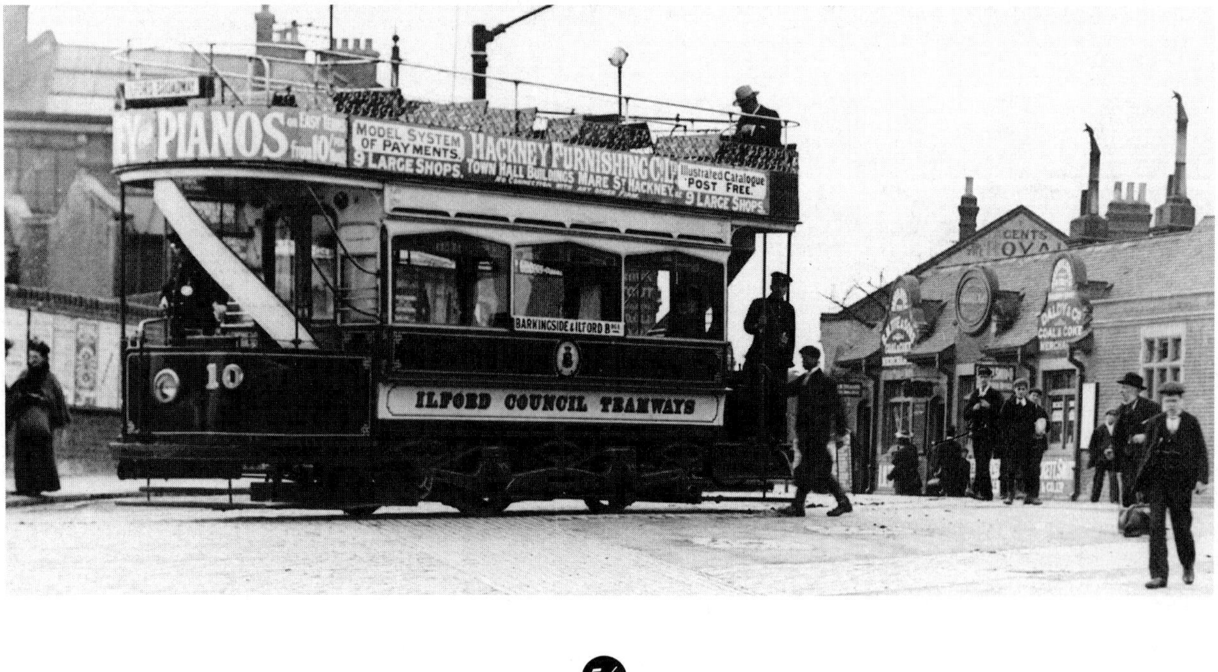

COUNTRY TRAMS

Almost a misnomer but many tram operators laid lines out into the country either to carry holiday makers or in the hope (often fulfilled) that development would follow.

▲ Camborne & Redruth, the furthest west of all mainland tramways, just after the opening 7 November 1902. The uniforms, as befits their responsible jobs, are of a very military cut. The 'Gaffer' is very obvious! [D.H. Johnzon]

◂ Queens Arms, Old Glossop, with car 3 resplendent in dark green and primrose paintwork. The date is 21 August 1903 and what we see is the inaugural service. No-one (except those planning it) were to know that in eleven years most of these youths would be off to a war and many of the girls having lost their men would end up as 'old maids'. Never wholly viable, the tramway closed at 11 p.m. on 24 December 1927; all the staff being then sacked, with severance - or redundancy pay - of just £5, about two weeks' pay.

▲ I have to confess I do not know the exact location of this photograph although I think it is near Howdon. Certainly it is on the main line from Gosforth to Wallsend of the Tyneside Tramways and Tramroads Company who built this tram route over the trackbed of the Coxlodge Colliery waggonway.

◂ Gosport and Fareham tramway in idyllic country surroundings at Hoe Ford, Fareham, shortly after the opening of their service. Totally useless country for tram working of course, although no doubt they carried passengers to and from the Inn on the right. This was a rare example of a road side stretch of tramway.

◂ During the Christmas period, December 1906, the lines of the erstwhile Wakefield & District Light Railway (albeit by then part of the Yorkshire (West Riding) Tramways company's network) suffered from heavy continuous driving snowfalls. Two cars were trapped near Horbury with at least half a mile of track being blocked despite men working all night to clear the road. Country conditions indeed! [K. Jenkinson].

A CALL TO ARMS

It is an unpleasant fact of 21st century life that any good part of Britain's history is denigrated by today's wretched, snivelling, "good thinkers". The patriotism of men, often from awful slums, poorly treated by employers and their 'betters' alike, during the first world war should never be denied. All of these trams were decorated by the staff in their own time and at their own expense. There is, however, an unfortunate side effect of these recruiting drives because many tramwaymen themselves volunteered and despite employment of many women, services had to be curtailed and maintenance minimalized; many tramway concerns were never to recover.

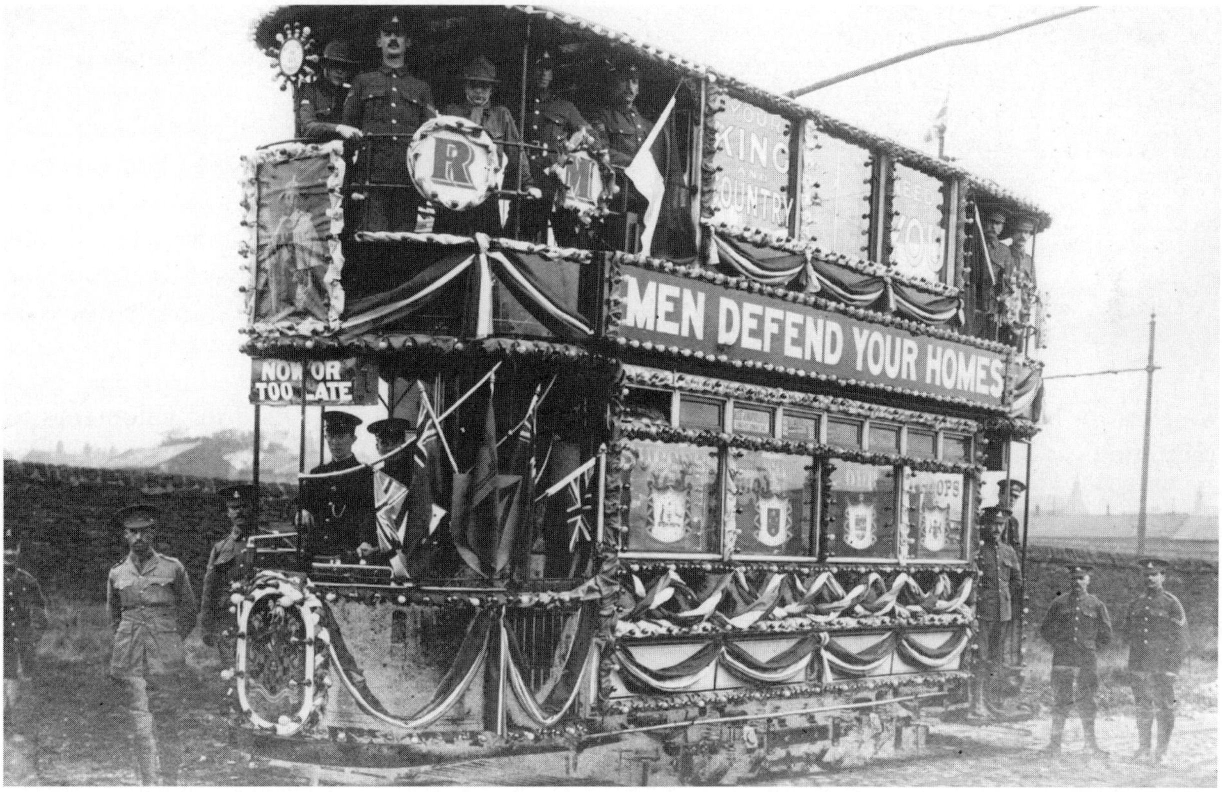

▲ "Your King and Country need You" and "Success to our Troops" are two of the less obvious slogans on this car. I must confess the tram is so well concealed beyond that it is in the north of England, I do not know the location.

▶ If this is the reverse side of the tram above, or its sister, then both are Halifax trams in November 1914. In the top car servicemen are visible. In the lower car only the Halifax civilians are to be seen, they may well be the employees who decorated the car.

▲ Not to be outdone Huddersfield ran a recruiting car during 1914/15.

▼ Dumbarton's tram called for volunteers to join the 9th Argyll & Sutherland Highlanders in 1915.

TRAMS IN COLOUR

POSTCARDS

Picture postcards of the type and quality shown here, so-called 'topographicals' were initially very stilted due to the long time exposures required even into the 1890s, but more lively scenes began to be possible in 1900, its generally said that their heyday was from 1904 to the end of the first world war although my own collection of tram and coach (char-a-banc) cards contains many excellent 'Real Photograph' cards printed 1919-1925.

Colour film did not exist, so either oil or watercolour paintings were commissioned or the originals were painstakingly hand coloured prior to printing. Much of this work before the war was carried out in Saxony (Germany) where their equipment was more advanced.

▲ Laxey, Isle of Man. Issued by Boots the Chemist. Details of a lost way of life over 100 years ago.

▼ Great Western Road, Glasgow "Chromotyped in Hessen [Germany]" A remarkably delicate scene with the overhead clearly visible.

▲ Market Place, Nottingham. The multi-wired pole must have been a nightmare to maintain and highly stressed.

▶ Guildhall and High Street, Exeter. The casual way pedestrians are ambling across the road is a long-gone facet of life, as is the errand boy. Posted in Middlesex, 28 December 1910.

▼ The horses' condition says it all really. Posted in York 8.45 p.m., 6 November 1905.

▲ Sent from Blackpool at 4.30 p.m. on 28 June 1905. The message simply reads "Will be back tomorrow morning all being well." The intended destination was Hulme, Manchester. The tram with very odd 'fudged' overhead equipment is one of the Dreadnought class. Long shadows and long skirts.

▶ Without comment... Posted 9p.m. 18 July 1906 from Taunton to Honiton. "Printed in Germany".

▼ A short lived narrow (3'6") gauge tramway, Kirkaldy's system operated from 1903 to 1931 when the Corporation sold out to the bus company W. Alexander for £27,000 down and 21 years at £2,000 p.a. But a marvellously clear card.

▲ The poles are real - heaven only knows why West Hartlepool chose this design but once again the overhead is missing. It was 8.30 but a.m. or p.m.? A rather sad message is written on this card posted, 25 May 1918.

▶ "Lovely place, lovely weather, everything lovely" says Clara, writing to Huddersfield in 1919. Whitley Bay can be beautiful and can also be wracked by incredible winds and driving snow. That remains but the trams are gone, alas.

▼ An unusual photograph showing not only a tram in Gloucester but in Northgate Street. The problems with narrow roads can be seen all too well. I like the shop keeper on the right sweeping his pavement.

UP THE AXE - SEATON & DISTRICT TRAMWAY COMPANY

Running from Seaton to Colyton via understated countryside this 2'9" gauge tramway started life at Eastbourne in 1954 but after some vicissitudes was re-located to Seaton in 1970 and has (thankfully) never looked back. The 3 miles or so journey to Colyton is an experience to be tried again and again and it is pleasant to state that at least one tram capable of carrying wheelchairs is in service at all times.

CRICH TRAMWAY MUSEUM

This is, of course, the oldest tramway museum in the United Kingdom and as a corollary is run very efficiently providing a full service of tramcars throughout the days they are open. There is also a static museum, excellent bookshop and a very helpful research library. One of Crich's claims is that their trackwork incorporates many varieties of road surface giving a pleasant effect.

EAST ANGLIAN TRANSPORT MUSEUM

The East Anglian Transport Museum, Carlton Colville, 3 miles west of Lowestoft is one of the older museums in the transport field (founded 1965) and has two great advantages - all the staff are enthusiasts, unpaid 'professionals' who enjoy their hobby-cum-work and the museum has an immense variety of different forms of transport on show in addition to trams and trolleybuses - steam rollers, a narrow gauge people-carrying railway, buses, coaches, lorries, cycles, stationary (barn) engines ... and a London taxi. And a bookshop. And a cafe.

▸ A typical scene in 1999.

▾ Carlton Colville by night. A spectacular and almost forgotten facet of tram and trolleybus operation; on a wet night with only a few pedestrians and cars about on the roads this was one of the pleasures of working in public transport that is recaptured every September at Carlton Colville.

▲ 1999. Some of the boskage has been removed and a new housing estate built behind the trams since this photograph was taken, greatly enhancing the effect.

▲ Spectacular. 1858 was built in 1930 for the London County Council by English Electric, Preston, and ran in London until the last day of tramway operation in July 1952. [East Anglian Transport Museum]

▼ Scenes in a museum do not come much more beautiful than this: Maidstone Corporation 1953 trolleybus and Blackpool Corporation (who built the body) 1927 tram. The gift and bookshop always welcomes visitors with some decent bits and pieces. [East Anglian Transport Museum]

▼ A strange Public House sign at nearby Gorleston-on-Sea. Neither Great Yarmouth nor Lowestoft had steam trams but it is a super painting of what might have been.

CONCERTS, CAROLS AND CAPERS

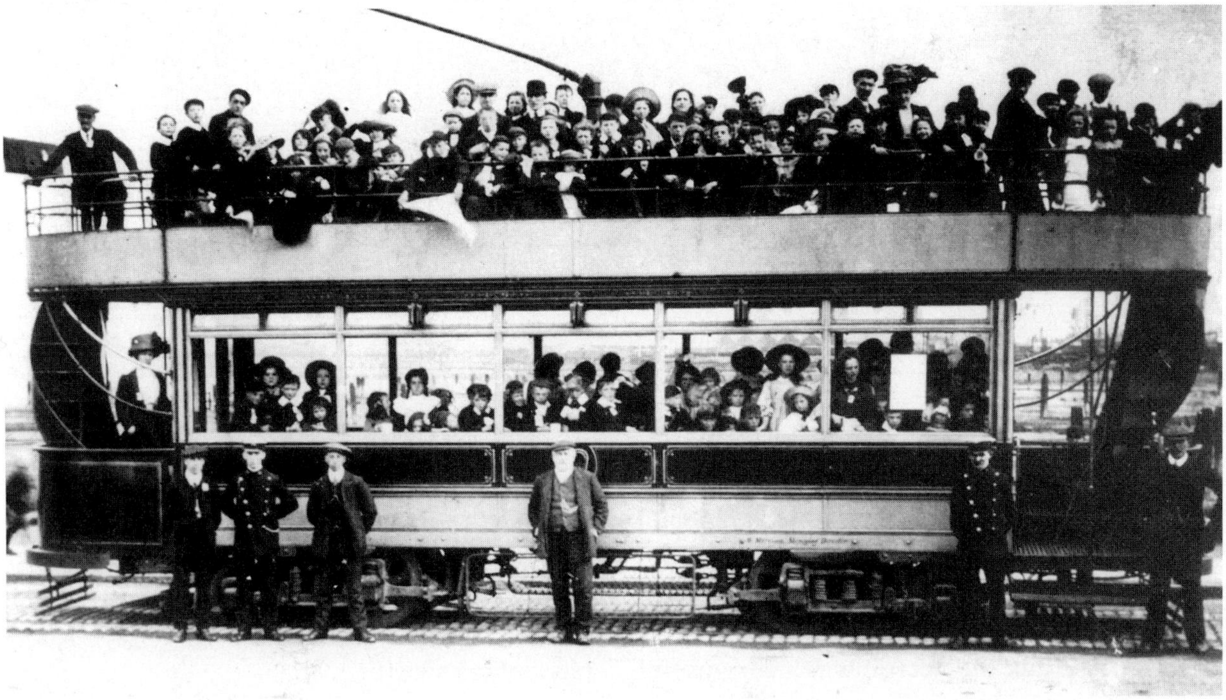

▲ A school outing no doubt and pre-1914 without question. The Barrow-in-Furness tramcar is no longer new so I would guess 1910 or so.

▼ 28 August 1909. Church Gresley Trinity Parish Church's Sunday School outing. Blasé people today have no idea how much care was taken to attend Sunday School for the 20-odd weeks prior to such a trip and the excitement it engendered. Burton & Ashby Light Railway trams.

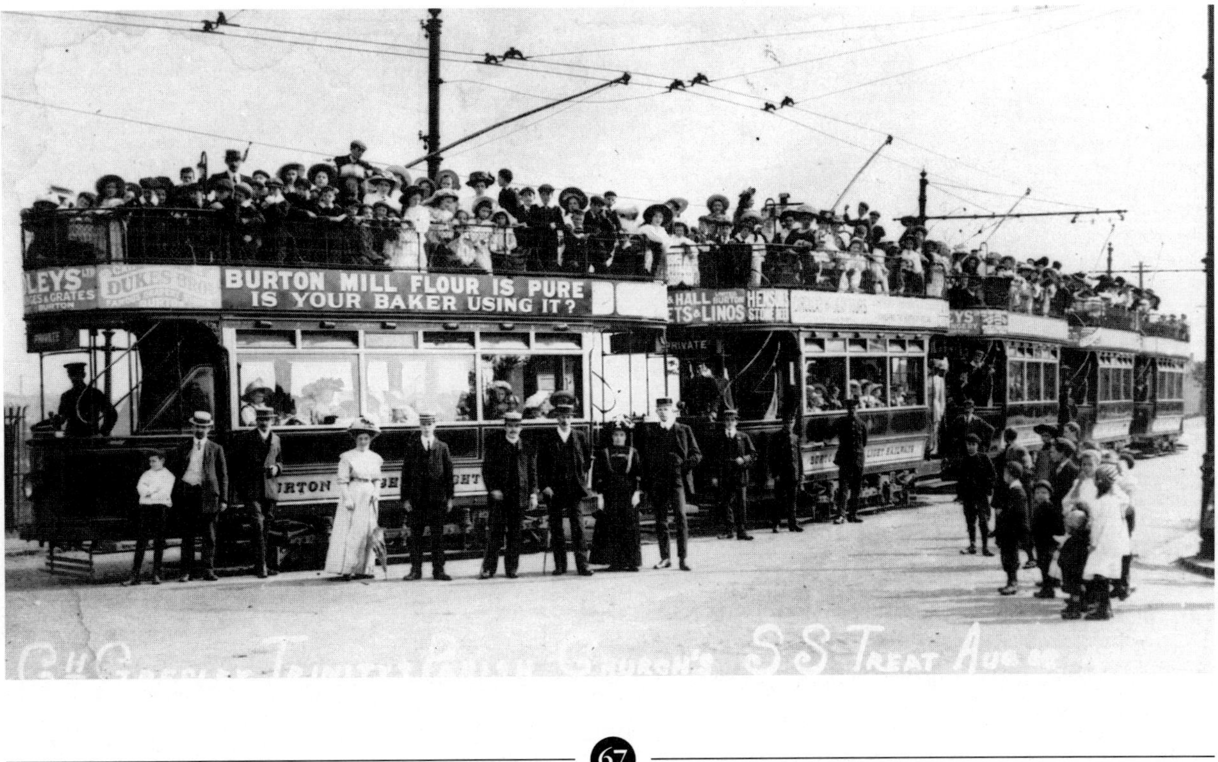

▲ The story of electric tram services in the Portsmouth district is confusing. There was some excuse as at various times the streets saw an oil fired steam tram, a clockwork assisted horse tram and, on the pier, a sort-of-tram propelled by sails. All rather fairground stuff but for these folk the 'lectric was a very useful means of travel that lasted until 1936.This card is entitled "After the Fair, Portsdown Hill" - it would rain!

▼ Anytime almost anywhere on a Saturday. 179 was a Birmingham Corporation Tramways car of 1906 seating by the 1920s, 49 but carrying 70 plus after football matches, as here! 179 was scrapped in 1939 but before this I can count fourteen trams waiting - say 1,000 passengers worth!

A great feature of the heyday of Britain's tramways was dressing up cars for celebrations, or - I feel - for the sheer fun of it.

▲ Guernsey. Battle of the Flowers. [R.W. Kidner]

▶ Rochdale. 1918. "Peace and goodwill to all men".

▼ Newcastle 1926. Lord Mayor's Appeal for Newcastle Royal Infirmary.

▲ Birmingham. Self evident.

▸ Middlesborough. Postcard 1925. The "H" and "T" in Help The Hospitals are red bulbs and ortho film does not treat them well.

▸ Yorkshire Woollen District.
- Fearon - Wines & Spirits
- Popplewell - confectionery
- B & A Meat Co. - butcher
- Prudential - Insurance
- Thompson-Builders Merchants
- Wattsman's Tailoring
- Walter Sykes - Sweets?

are among those advertising. Do any survive?

▲ Blackpool. Still the best 1926.

▼ Halifax. Safety first at Pellon Lane, 1936.

▲ Dublin. Although not in Britain, the captions are very amusing. My favourite being on the left dashplate.

▼ Metropolitan Electric Tramways advertising partly route 32 (finished September 1937) but mostly a celebration of Wood Green having received their charter as an independent Borough. It meant quite a lot in those 20th century days. [London Transport]

US, THAT IS TRAM STAFF (PAST & PRESENT)

Despite working in passenger transport for most of my earning life, it is a matter of truth and regret that I knew very few of my colleagues well, the very transient nature of this employment precluded doing so. But in homage to the tram staff of bygone days I offer the following illustrations.

▲ Reading 1919. Second row are 'Inspectoresses'. The third and fifth rows contain conductresses and lady drivers. (Please note this was how they were described by the driver at the right hand end of the second row!). [H.E. Jordon]

▼ Bradford 1920s. Try 20 mph (36 kph) in those conditions. A test of man and machine.

▼ London County Council Tramways. The motorman's badge (222) is very prominent. [LCCTT]

▲ Newcastle. A car of the series 111-130 built by Hurst Nelson and shiny new in 1901.

▼ Burnley Tramways in their first decade before the Great War. Pillbox type hats on two men.

▲ Peterborough. Official photograph to mark the departure of the Manager, Mr. Blake. 1923. Lady staff are still present, most concerns sacked theirs in 1919.

▼ Newcastle again. 1950s. The reality of the job. [A.D. Packer]

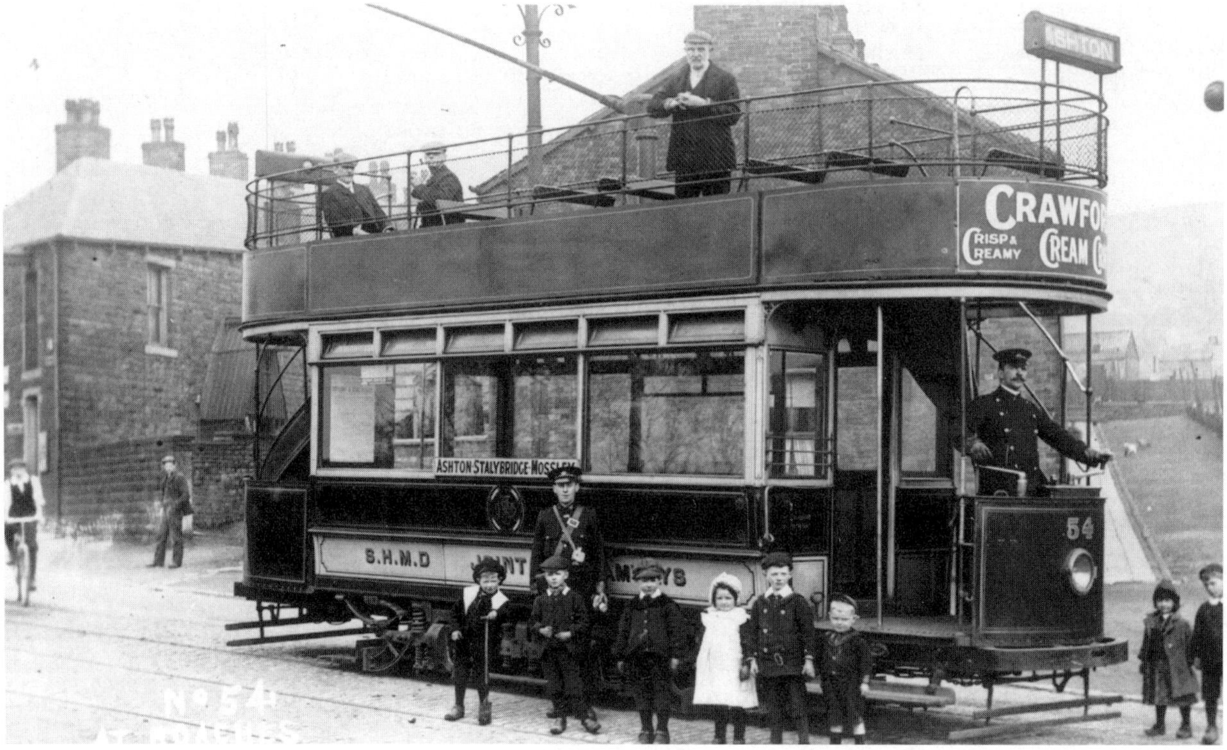

▲ Stalybridge, Hyde, Mossley & Dukinfield Tramways and Electricity Board car in 1907. (I had to put the SHMD Board's name in full - it is so traditional).

▼ Poole & District Electric Traction Company's shed, Upper Parkstone. The Manager, E.H. Mottram, is on the extreme left.

▲ A contemporary press report stated: "When one remembers the drunken men who get on the tramcars and the horrid language they use it makes me shudder to think of young women as conductors". Perhaps so but most operators were glad enough of them after the carnage in the trenches drew away more male staff. But although this is a Doncaster car c.1916, the Inspectoress looks similar to and as smart as many of the WRAF personnel I knew thirty years later.

▲ Devonport & District pre-1914.

▲ We know she was 'Lily' but where?

▼ Bristol, Fishponds Terminus 1918. Mrs. Curry (nee Lilian Bailey) was one of the first clippies employed. The girls lasted from 1917-1921. [Peter Davey]

▼ York 1916 and an all-girl crew.

▲ Bath Tramways. Women drivers and conductresses; the few men were often those invalided out of the army. [C.G. Maggs]

▼ Weston-super-Mare, Locking Road depot, 15 October 1909. The boys mostly worked the points or provided the parcels express delivery.

▲ Time in stasis. Burton & Ashby Light Railways. Swadlincote.

▼ Traditional tram. Traditional staff. But it is in Johannesburg. [B.T. Cooke]

▼ A delightful photograph (originally sepia-toned) of Glasgow Corporation Transport's Maintenance Car No.1. Built new in 1905 as the (Electrical) Mains Departments Cable Layer & Withdrawer. The upright design allowed this car to carry full size cable drums. It says it all regarding the condition of the road when we realize No.1 is standing on tram-rails.

▲ Glasgow, Dalmuir West terminus, 1 September 1962. [J.C. Gillham]

▼ This is what trams were all about - people. The line is Crosland Moor of the Huddersfield Corporation Tramways, opened 18 February 1901 and this car was delivered 1902.

BRIGHT LIGHTS

Trams "all lit up like galleons in the Moonlight" as someone put it.

▲ City of York Corporation Tramways. Coronation 1910.

◂ Blackpool being Blackpool. 1978.

▼ London Transport (ex.LCC) E3 Car at Savoy Street (Victoria Embankment) 1952. [J.C. Gillham]

▲ There is something poetic in the juxtaposition of a 'fancy' tram and the Co-op. This is Tramnik One built by Blackpool Corporation Transport using the frames of 1928 built Pantograph' car 168. Tramnik One entered service in 1961 and was quite literally astounding even to the more blasé visitors. Behind is the only survivor of Edinburgh's magnificent fleet, destroyed 1956. No.35, built at Shrubhill Depot in 1948; here providing a contrast with Tramnik.

BEAUTY IS IN THE EYE OF THE BEHOLDER

There has always been a swell of enthusiasm for tramways whether it be for their theoretical and practical advantages in the carrying of passengers, for the workmanship that went into the cars, or purely nostalgia for lost days. Unfortunately for no apparent quantifiable reason, the enthusiasts here are the same ones still involved today (although fewer as many have gone on Celestial Car 1 to Top Shed), if this continues without younger replacements it bodes badly for the future of museums like the East Anglian Tramway Society at Carlton Colville where there are only volunteers - enthusiasts all.

▲ Even in wartime some men gathered. Southampton, 4 April 1942, car 21.

▼ Light Railway Transport League (now LRTA), Blackpool 17 April 1949, Rigby Road Depot, car 208.

▲ This photograph shows a tramcar that is 'Special' in all sorts of ways. It was photographed in 1951 when in service with Leeds City Transport as their 446 but on hire to the Light Railway Transport League (now LRTA) whose members first knew it as No.132 of the Hull fleet, being home-built in 1910. But this saga does not stop there for nearly 100 years later 132/446 is still in existance at the Hull Transport Museum.

▼ Another enthusiasts day at Blackpool in 1989 with two modern styled but 'traditional' cars passing.

PLENTY OF ROOM INSIDE

▲ The West Ham car 125, home-built by the Corporation in 1925, photographed 1926. Slightly retouched originally, nonetheless the upholstered seating, dark (almost flat) varnished ceiling but quite modern lights look good for the period.

▼ Glasgow Corporation 779, a 1900 built 'Standard' (now preserved) photographed by J.C. Gillham as late as 1962. Full length brass ceiling rails, white painted roof structure, original and uncomfortable wooden seating for all the world as though it was still open topped. Naked light bulbs do not soften the appearance of the car. It was on a sister but rebuilt tram that a conductress, after incredulously watching a youth burning his initials on the refurbished leather covered seats with a cigarette, caught him such a ding around the lug with her ticket machine that we had to carry him to a nearby shop recess to recover. Calling the "Polis" meant canteen time wasted! [J.C. Gillham]

▲ ▼ Due to the steepness of the surrounding hills and the narrowness of the local roads Halifax trams were small and neat four-wheelers. 105 with the wooden seats was a single deck tram of archaic appearance both inside and out. 107 by contrast had a white enamelled ceiling, clock, polished brass and a route card which tells you not only where parks and connections are but also that shopping parcels can be forwarded free of charge and furthermore you should change at Southowram "for fresh air". [Both A.E. Dixon]

▲ Fleet no 90, a Hex dash Glasgow 'Standard' of 1920 seen 8 April 1958. [J.C. Gillham]

▼ 526, Round dash, monitor roofed 'Standard' of 1902. Photographed 14 September 1960. This car retained her wartime (1943) crush loading longitudinal seats until destroyed by fire at Dalmarnock Depot 1961. [J.C. Gillham]

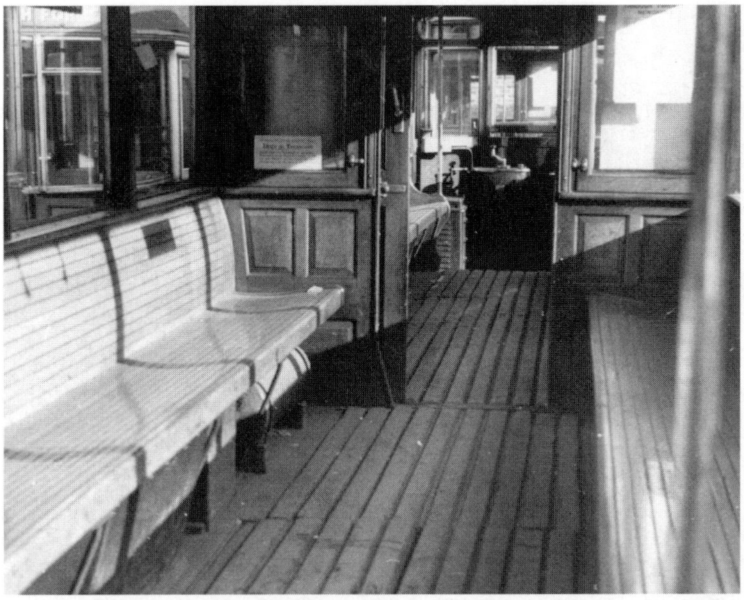

◂ Obviously the intended traffics on the line made a difference to their comfort. This car of the Gateshead & District fleet was photographed in March 1951; single deck but with the ability to uplift great numbers of standing passengers. [Alan B. Cross]

◂ 1290, 'Coronation' car of 1940. The conductress with her ticket machine is trying to hide under the stairs but was caught on film on 13 September 1961.
[J.C. Gillham]

▾ 1282, preserved Coronation of 1940.

THE ACCIDENT AT HALIFAX - 1 JULY 1906

Three views of the same accident which occurred in Halifax, 1 July 1906, when car 94 ran away out of control down New Bank before overturning on North Bridge. These photographs (one a commercial card, the others are 'snaps') show more clearly than words how little of a tram was supported by the truck and why 'jazzing', 'tailwag' and 'oscillation' could be quite frightening to an upstairs passenger - on the worst trackwork the tram body would lurch from corner to corner, swaying left to right and end to end. This was particularly noticeable on narrow gauge lines (Halifax had a track gauge of 3'6"/107 cm) and explains to some degree why the Board of Trade initially disliked both covered tops and enclosed vestibules on these tall, slender cars. An author is supposed to be totally dispassionate but I find the photographs of this accident particularly poignant, not because of the casualties (two killed, eleven injured) but because Halifax and its people have changed so much since July 1906. Shawls, clogs, caps, bowler hats, trams, tram rails, overhead wiring, gas lamps, granite setts, have all gone. I wonder what life the millgirls in the foreground led?

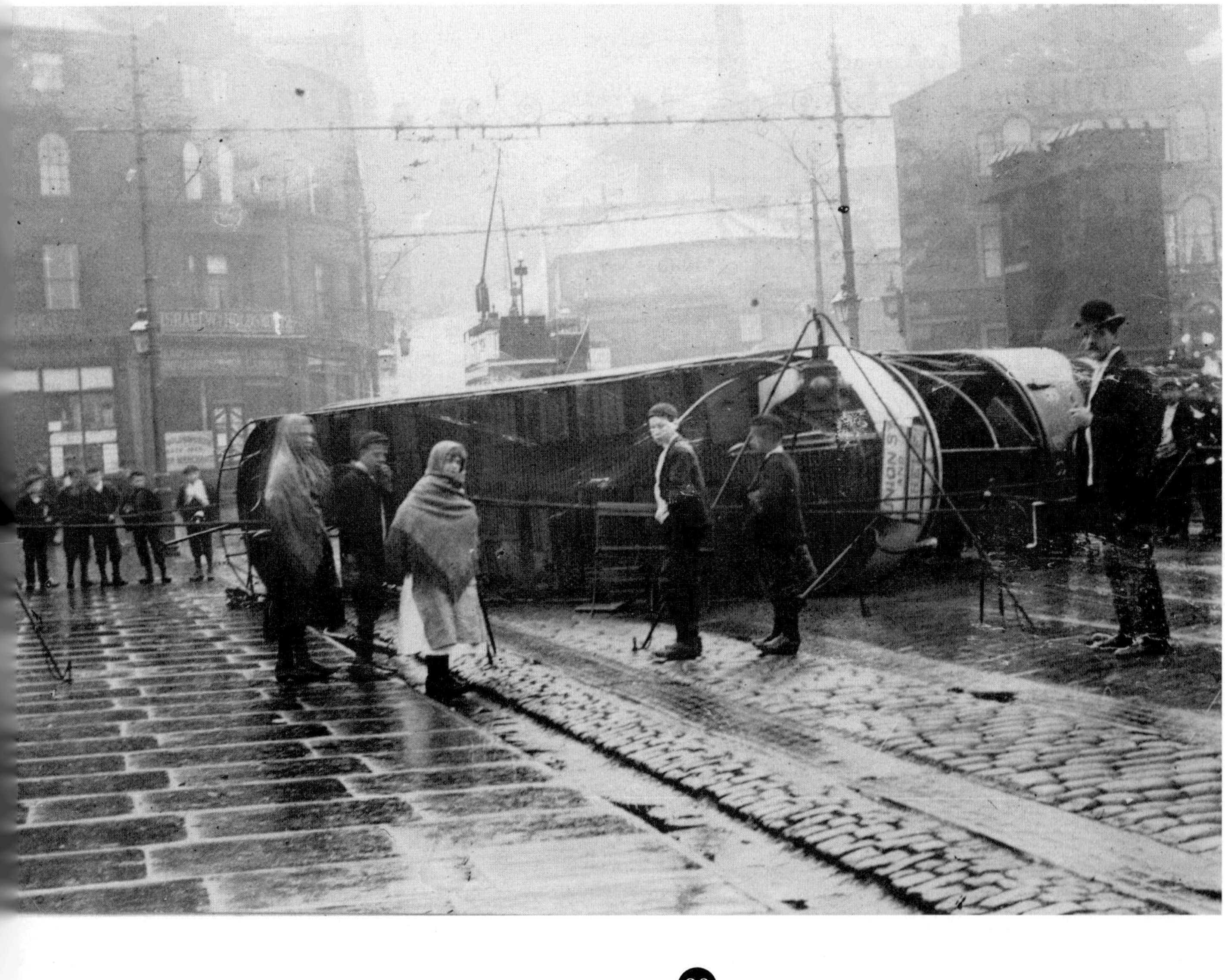

UNION ST
AND
SHELF

NESTLE'S
MILK
The Richest in Cream
ALL ROUTES VIA NORTH BRIDGE
TRAM SMASH, HALIFAX, JULY 1ST 1906.

GOING, GOING, GONE

The going of British trams was poignant and whatever face they may have officially put on it town planners everywhere could hardly conceal their glee as city after city abandoned the streetcar, one hopes they enjoyed their cosy time with the developers - I doubt if they cared about the men and women left to find other employment, often after 30 or 40 years 'at the handles'. This was Oldham.
[A.D. Packer Collection]

▲ "Trams have ceased to be a luxury and are now a necessity of town life ... whether they have come to stay permanently is another matter. Possibly ... they may be superceded by the more humble motorbus ...". This appeared in the Keighley News shortly after the electrification of their service on 12 October 1904. Twenty years and a world war later the trackwork was in appalling condition and here we see a neat, if man-powered, rail carrier in use, recovering rails on the road between Keighley and Utley prior to replacement of the trams with trolleybuses; the last car running 17 December 1924.

▼ One time West Ham car 36 later LT 246 is seen at the end of its days in 1937. Originally built in 1905 by G.F. Milnes, this class was rebuilt by the West Ham Corporation workshops in the early 1920s. Standard Brush four wheel trucks of 7' (2.13m) wheelbase were used and Westinghouse controllers. In the foreground is a Hurst Nelson truck withdrawn from under an ex-class "M" car. To me the saddest part of scenes like this lies in the fact that generations of men and women had cleaned and polished this car every night, men and women had driven it, and collected fares as it moved along, and hundreds of thousands of busy, busy men, women and children had ridden on it. What price pride in doing a job well? Even for a tram life is ephemeral. [Collection A.D. Packer]

THE (VERY) END

I do not know what is more poignant - the shell of car 96 at Charlton scrapyard in 1952, the burning of B.C.T. cars two years later or the awful finality of closed doors and disused tracks but...

[Page 95, R.C. Crombleholme]

DRIVE IN & SHUT GATES
KEEP
DOOR
SHUT
PRIVATE
NO UNAUTHORISED
PERSONS.

LIFE AFTER DEATH

THE BLACK COUNTRY LIVING MUSEUM (OPENED 6TH AUGUST 1980)

▲ Wolverhampton Tramways Company standard gauge car No.23 restored by the British Horse Tram Enthusiasts. Built by the Falcon works as late as 1892. [Eric Birch]

▼ Wolverhampton Tram 49 of 1908, alongside Wolverhampton trolleybus 433, a 1946 Sunbeam 'W' with a 1960 Roe body. Here 49 is awaiting varnishing. [Eric Birch]

INDEX

RECENT BOOKS BY THE SAME AUTHOR

Coaching Cavalcade, Brewin Books, 1991

Midbus, Brewin Books, 1992

Britain's Motor Buses, Brewin Books, 1993

The Glory of Electric Trams, The Oakwood Press, 1993

PSV Panorama, Brewin Books, 1994

The Canals of Britain, Breedon Books, 1994

Building Britain's Canals, Brewin Books, 1998

Aspects of Buses, The Oakwood Press 2003

A History of the British Steam Tram Vol.1, Adam Gordon, 2004

It is rumoured the author has a tram stashed away; I hope any resemblance between him and the elderly gentleman lies entirely in the cartoonist's eye. [Steve Hallam]